Deploying For Success: Advanced Strategies, Techniques, And Design In DevOps

Description

Whether you are new or experienced, this tailor-made guide navigates the complexities of modern development, automation, and cloud technology.

Let us start by creating a flexible workspace within AWS using the power of tools like Terraform and Terragrunt. Next, understand how to set up secure networks in AWS with Virtual Private Cloud (VPC) configurations. Then, go a step further into Amazon's Elastic Kubernetes Service (EKS) to explore how to work with containerized applications.

As you get better at the basics, you will also learn about making Docker images work better and creating setups that are all set for production ready. You will also explore ways to deploy your work, from small local setups to a production ready environment.

This book is designed to take complex ideas and make them simple to understand and apply – your perfect companion on the journey to becoming a DevOps expert.

Target Audience

This book is proposed for those seeking clarity and proficiency in modern DevOps practices. It is crafted with a clear purpose—to serve as the definitive resource for individuals who are eager to learn the core architecture and orchestration techniques in the realm of DevOps.

It is designed to equip readers with a comprehensive toolbox of basic and advanced tools, showing the techniques from a day-to-day DevOps perspective.

In contrast to conventional methods, this book introduces innovative approaches that have the potential to completely transform the way you manage deployments. It encompasses the most current techniques and strategies, designed to elevate your DevOps abilities, and ensure that your deployment processes are smooth and effective. From inventive design principles to advanced deployment strategies, this book provides you with the essential resources to fine-tune your application delivery pipeline.

About the Author

Meet Lidor Ettinger, an accomplished DevOps engineer with a specialization in Continuous Delivery and Cloud infrastructure. With a comprehensive grasp of systems development, Lidor has taken the helm as the lead implementer of intricate multilayered systems in dynamic orchestration production environments. Notably, he has made substantial contributions to the Apache open-source project while consistently sharing his wealth of practical insights through technology blogs, illuminating his problem-solving journey and solution-driven approaches. His diverse technical passions naturally guided him to the ever-evolving domain of DevOps, where he has carved his niche and continues to thrive.

As a DevOps engineer, Lidor wears many hats. He is your team's collaborator extraordinaire, tackling various projects with a grin. From scripting magic to nurturing automated systems, he is all about making things work smoother. Driven by his passion and can-do attitude, Lidor is on a mission to discover inventive ways to supercharge infrastructure.

Special shoutout to my incredible wife, Elizabeth – your unwavering support fuels my creativity. And a big thank you to the awesome folks and companies that have shaped my journey. Your trust empowers me to embrace the job I adore!

Navigating the Path to Success

The demand for advanced deployment techniques and design in the field of DevOps is rapidly growing. Over the past few years, there has been a surge in publications and technologies centered around these principles. With this book, you will gain invaluable insights, practical knowledge, and expert guidance to navigate the evolving landscape of DevOps roadmap.

Equip yourself with the tools and techniques to meet the rising demand and make a lasting impact in the world of software engineering and infrastructure management.

Tech List

This comprehensive book uses a selection of powerful open-source tools to boost your understanding and proficiency in the world of software deployment.

Throughout the book, we will delve into essential technologies such as Docker Engine and Docker Compose, enabling you to learn the process of building local images and running them before applying to production environments. Additionally, we will explore key aspects of Kubernetes, including deployment strategies like Blue-Green Deployment, Canary Deployments etc.

To showcase diverse deployment methodologies, we will delve into Amazon Web Services (AWS) to demonstrate how to effectively run infrastructure in the cloud. You will gain invaluable experience in deploying applications in EKS.

Moreover, we will explore the importance of Terraform, a tool that allows you to create infrastructure using code. But that is not all – we will also use Terragrunt, which acts like a smart wrapper for Terraform. It includes additional tools to assist us in avoiding repetition and keeping our infrastructure neat and tidy.

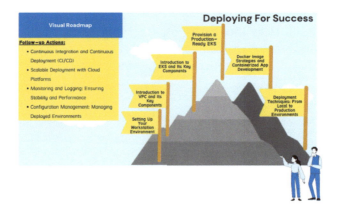

Table of Contents

Chapter Details

Chapter 1: Setting Up Your Workstation Environment

Description: In this chapter, we will configure our workstation environment in the AWS cloud to create a consistent and isolated setup that is accessible to everyone. By choosing a cloud-based workstation, we can ensure a stable and standardized environment, enabling us to provide you with a reliable workstation based on our instructions.

Topics to be covered:

- Provision a VPC using Cloud9:
    - Set up your workstation environment by creating a dedicated EC2 instance that functions as a secure gateway, providing access to your private instances within a VPC.
- Provisioning Resources in a Private Cloud Environment:
    - Connect and manage an EKS cluster in private subnets using AWS's Cloud9
- Bugs and fixes:
    - Guidelines for managing bugs.

Chapter 2: Introduction to VPC and Its Key Components

Description: In this chapter, we will explore the foundational concepts of a Virtual Private Cloud (VPC) in AWS. We will discuss the significance of various components within a VPC, including subnets, route tables, internet gateways, NAT gateways, and security groups. Additionally, we will examine the relationships between these resources and their role in creating a secure and isolated network environment for your AWS infrastructure.

Topics to be covered:

- The Importance of Infrastructure as Code:
  - Discover the significance of Infrastructure as Code (IaC) and its associated DevOps tools, such as Terraform and Terragrunt, for automating the provisioning and management of cloud resources.
- Strategic Infrastructure Design and Planning:
  - Explore the process of designing and planning your infrastructure, including identifying the necessary resources and modules required for launching your infrastructure.
- An in-depth exploration of the Terragrunt resource - Overview and Deep Dive:
  - Take a closer look at the Terragrunt code block encompassing our VPC module along with all its dependencies for our practical hands-on session.
- Provisioning VPC with Terragrunt:
  - Let us kickstart the process by taking your first action and provisioning your VPC in the cloud.
- Exploring Storage Options on AWS:
  - Get to know the AWS storage options and their advantages in Cloud Computing.
- Create your Amazon EFS file system:
  - Set up an AWS EFS as a shared volume for infrastructure usage.

Chapter 3: Introduction to EKS and Its Key Components

Description: In this chapter, we will delve into the world of Amazon Elastic Kubernetes Service (EKS) and its essential components. We will use Terragrunt to explore the Infrastructure as Code (IaC) approach to provisioning an EKS cluster.

Topics to be covered:

- Overview of the EKS and its components:
  - Explore the ease of getting started with Amazon Elastic Kubernetes Service (EKS), including the creation of an EKS cluster, launching EC2 nodes or utilizing AWS Fargate for workload deployment, configuring Kubernetes tools, and managing workloads on the EKS cluster using familiar Kubernetes practices.
- Illustrating a Kubernetes Application in Action
  - Break down the structure of an application within Kubernetes.
- Navigating User Requests to Pods:
  - Visualize the journey of a user request to the cluster and its corresponding response.
- HPA in Kubernetes:
  - Explore Kubernetes' HorizontalPodAutoscaler (HPA), a dynamic tool that adjusts pod quantities within workloads to optimize resource utilization by scaling up during high demand and down during low demand.
- EKS : Terragrunt Module and Dependency Relationships:
  - Accelerate your cloud journey by deploying and scaling your infrastructure using Amazon Elastic Kubernetes Service (EKS) on your Virtual Private Cloud (VPC).
- Provisioning EKS with Terragrunt:
  - Continuing the provisioning journey: constructing an infrastructure with an orchestration playground environment.
- Check the cluster status:

- Establish a connection to our provisioned EKS cluster using Cloud9 (or "bastion") and check our cluster health.

Chapter 4: Provision a Production-Ready EKS

Description: In this chapter, we will guide you in constructing a production-ready EKS cluster, complete with EFS, Node Group, and nginx integration.

Topics to be covered:

- Introduction to the Node Group and its Terragrunt Configuration:
  - An Insight into the Node Group and its Terragrunt Setup
- Node Group Provisioning:
  - Establish an EKS managed node group within the VPC's private subnets, ensuring it is prepared to accommodate the deployment of our upcoming applications.
- Provisioning Metric Server:
  - Collecting metrics related to CPU and memory usage from applications to enhance our ability to observe application performance.
- Provisioning a Network Load Balancer with the NGINX Ingress Controller:
  - Continuing the provisioning journey: Constructing an infrastructure with an orchestration playground environment.
- Domain Certificate: Creating a self-signed certificate for SSL Termination:
  - Enabling Secure Routing: Creating a self-signed certificate for our services.
- Provisioning a Kubernetes dashboard:
  - Provision your first Kubernetes service, which will give you an overall observability about your cluster performance.

Chapter 5: Docker Image Strategies and Containerized App Development

Description: In this chapter, we will explore the significance of efficient build plans in DevOps, focusing on optimizing Docker image builds using single-stage and multi-stage approaches. It also delves into meticulous planning for containerized applications, highlighting its impact on successful deployments in a DevOps environment.

Topics to be covered:

- The Significance of Effective build in DevOps:
  - Optimize Docker image builds with single-stage and multi-stage approaches, along with .dockerignore file usage.
- Key aspects while building a containerized application:
  - Examine the importance of meticulous planning and the impact it has on the success of deployments in a DevOps environment.
- Overview of the Docker Image single-stage:
  - Discover the Dockerfile layers while creating a single stage.
- Overview of the Docker Image multi-stage:
  - Discover the Dockerfile layers while creating a multi-stage.
- Overview of the Docker Ignore file:
  - Discover the Docker Ignore file.
- Optimizing Builds with Efficient Cache Management:
  - Discover the strategic layering decisions in constructing a Dockerfile, which significantly accelerate image builds and play a vital role in improving build speeds by eliminating the need for redundant image reconstruction.
- Hands on: Building a docker image:
  - Build our Dockerfile locally.

Chapter 6: Deployment Strategies and Techniques - From Local to Production

Description: This chapter investigates the various deployment techniques employed in the transition from local development environments to production environments within the context of DevOps. It focuses on the strategies and considerations for successful and scalable deployments.

Topics to be covered:

- Run Docker on your local environment:
  - Start by running your Docker image locally to take the initial step of debugging and testing your first version before moving on to production.
- Get ready to explore deployment strategies and techniques:
  - Explore deployment techniques! Get ready to learn about Blue/Green, Canary deployments, Helm, and Terraform strategies.
- Deploy your first application in EKS using Helm Chart:
  - Enable access to your application within the EKS cluster via the preconfigured load balancer.
- Configure a Canary deployment:
  - Implement a canary deployment and distribute traffic between different versions of your deployment.

Chapter 7: Wrapping Up and Staying Engaged

Topics to be covered:

- Clean Up the Infrastructure
- Deploy the entire infrastructure with a single command
- Stay Connected

Code reference for your convenience

Reference	URL
#1	https://github.com/naturalett/terragrunt
#2	https://registry.terraform.io/modules/terraform-aws-modules/vpc/aws/5.0.0
#3	https://registry.terraform.io/modules/terraform-aws-modules/eks/aws/19.14.0
#4	https://github.com/naturalett/terragrunt/blob/main/infra/03-eks/update_kubeconfig.sh
#5	https://us-east-1.console.aws.amazon.com/ec2/home?region=us-east-1#AutoScalingGroups
#6	https://github.com/naturalett/maven-workshop
#7	https://console.aws.amazon.com/cloud9/home#
#8	https://www.calculator.net/ip-subnet-calculator.html
#9	https://github.com/naturalett/terragrunt/blob/main/modules/kubernetes-dashboard/kubernetes-dashboard.tf
#10	https://hub.docker.com/

Chapter 1:
Setting Up Your Workstation Environment

In this chapter, we will tackle the process of provisioning a VPC using Cloud9, which involves setting up a dedicated EC2 instance to serve as a secure gateway, granting access to private instances within the VPC.

Next, we will provision resources within a private cloud environment. This will include steps to establish and manage an EKS cluster located within private subnets, all orchestrated through AWS's Cloud9 platform.

Finally, we will address common issues that can come up during the provisioning, such as handling bugs and fixes.

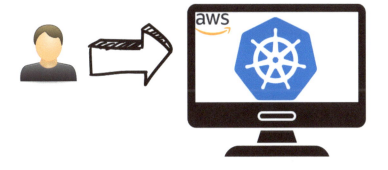

Provision a VPC using Cloud9

To prepare for provisioning the VPC, EKS, and other infrastructure resources later in the book, you have two options. You can either use your local machine to set up the cloud infrastructure, or you can launch an instance or Cloud9 environment that enables you to connect to the cloud and perform the necessary provisioning tasks.

At first, our journey will begin with the necessity of a VPC to lay the foundation for constructing our infrastructure resources.

In order to achieve this, our initial step will involve provisioning a Cloud9 instance within the default VPC that AWS offers. The default VPC will serve as the initial setup to generate the new VPC of our book. In this manner, we ensure that we create resources within our VPC, which enables us to continue building our infrastructure smoothly.

Step 1 – Access the Amazon Cloud9 (Follow-up reference #7)

Step 2 – Launch the environment on the default VPC (Give your Cloud9 name: **dev-vpc**)

Step 3 – Execute each of the provided commands listed in the table below.

Description	Commands

Configure AWS	`export AWS_ACCESS_KEY_ID=<AWS_ACCESS_KEY_ID>`
	
	`export AWS_SECRET_ACCESS_KEY=<AWS_SECRET_ACCESS_KEY>`

Export Terraform environment variables	```export BUCKET="devops-workshop-$(uuidgen | tr "[:upper:]" "[:lower:]")"```
	
	```export ACCOUNT_ID=""```

Create a Bucket to store Terraform states	```aws s3api create-bucket --bucket "${BUCKET}"```
	
	```aws s3api put-bucket-tagging --bucket $BUCKET --tagging '{"TagSet": [{"Key": "workshop", "Value": "devops"}]}'```

Install Terragrunt	```wget https://github.com/gruntwork-io/terragrunt/releases/download/v0.50.3/terragrunt_linux_amd64```
	
	```sudo chmod +x terragrunt_linux_amd64```
	
	```sudo mv terragrunt_linux_amd64 /usr/bin/terragrunt```

Install Terraform	```wget https://releases.hashicorp.com/terraform/1.5.5/terraform_1.5.5_linux_amd64.zip```
	
	```unzip terraform_1.5.5_linux_amd64.zip```

	`sudo chmod +x terraform`
	
	`sudo mv terraform /usr/bin/terraform`

Clone Terragrunt Project	`mkdir -p workstation`
	
	`cd workstation`
	
	`git clone https://github.com/naturalett/terragrunt.git`
	
	`cd terragrunt`
	
	`terragrunt init && cd infra/01-vpc && terragrunt apply`

Provisioning Resources in a Private Cloud Environment

Let us set up a Cloud9 workspace in the newly created VPC. This will be our primary workstation, allowing us to create resources in our private subnets and connect to our EKS Cluster.

Step 1 – Access the Amazon Cloud9 (Follow-up reference #7)

Step 2 – Launch the environment on the precreated VPC (Give your Cloud9 name: **dev-infra**)

Step 3 – Execute each of the provided commands listed in the table below.

Description	Commands

Configure AWS	`export AWS_ACCESS_KEY_ID=<AWS_ACCESS_KEY_ID>`
	
	`export AWS_SECRET_ACCESS_KEY=<AWS_SECRET_ACCESS_KEY>`

Export Terraform environment variables that you have already created previously while Provision a	`sudo yum install jq -y`
	
	`cat <<'EOF' >> get_bucket.sh`
	
	`for bucket in $(aws s3api list-buckets | jq -r '.Buckets[].Name'); do`
	
	`    tags=$(aws s3api get-bucket-tagging --bucket $bucket`

21

Description	Commands

VPC using Cloud9	```
	2>/dev/null
		jq -r '.TagSet[] |
		select(.Key == "workshop" and
		.Value == "devops")')
		
		    if [-n "$tags"]; then
		
		        echo "$bucket"
		
		        exit 0
		
		    fi
		
		done
		
		EOF
		
		export BUCKET=$(bash
		get_bucket.sh)
		
		export ACCOUNT_ID=""
		``

Install Terragrunt	``` wget https://github.com/gruntwork- io/terragrunt/releases/download/v 0.50.3/terragrunt_linux_amd64 sudo chmod +x terragrunt_linux_amd64 sudo mv terragrunt_linux_amd64 /usr/bin/terragrunt ```

Description	Commands
| Install Terraform | ```
wget
https://releases.hashicorp.com/te
rraform/1.5.5/terraform_1.5.5_lin
ux_amd64.zip

unzip
terraform_1.5.5_linux_amd64.zip

sudo chmod +x terraform

sudo mv terraform
/usr/bin/terraform
``` |
| Install Kubectl | ```
curl -LO
https://storage.googleapis.com/ku
bernetes-
release/release/v1.23.6/bin/linux
/amd64/kubectl

chmod +x kubectl

sudo mv kubectl
/usr/local/bin/kubectl
``` |
| Install Helm | ```
curl -L
https://git.io/get_helm.sh | bash
-s -- --version v3.8.2
``` |
| Install awscli V2 | ```
curl
"https://awscli.amazonaws.com/aws
``` |

Description	Commands

	`cli-exe-linux-x86_64.zip" -o "awscliv2.zip"`
	
	`unzip awscliv2.zip`
	
	`sudo ./aws/install`

Install docker-compose	`sudo curl -L "https://github.com/docker/compose/releases/download/1.23.2/docker-compose-$(uname -s)-$(uname -m)" -o /usr/local/bin/docker-compose`
	
	`sudo chmod +x /usr/local/bin/docker-compose`

Clone Terragrunt project	`mkdir -p workstation`
	
	`cd workstation`
	
	`git clone https://github.com/naturalett/terragrunt.git`

Keep in mind

The EKS cluster has been provisioned in private subnets, which means direct connection from your local machine is not possible (please refer to the VPC architecture for a reminder). To establish a connection, you would typically need a VPN service solution. However, in this book, we are demonstrating an alternative approach using AWS's Cloud9 service. We are launching Cloud9 within our precreated VPC, allowing us to connect and manage the cluster from AWS.

Allow Access to EKS for the CIDR

Since our EKS is hosted on private subnets, external access to the cluster is restricted. To connect to the cluster, we use a Cloud9 instance within the same VPC (private subnet). However, to enable this connectivity, we might have to configure an inbound rule in the EKS security group.

Follow these steps:

- Access the Amazon EKS console by visiting https://console.aws.amazon.com/eks/home#/clusters
- Navigate to Networking -> Cluster security group and select the Additional security groups
- Add a new inbound rule with the following details:
- Type: All traffic
- Source: 10.106.0.0/16 (the CIDR of the VPC where the EKS is hosted)

By adding this inbound rule, we ensure that only the specified CIDR range within our VPC can access the EKS cluster, allowing the Cloud9 instance to establish a secure connection.

Bugs and fixes

terragrunt init -reconfigure

While provisioning resources with Terragrunt, there could be situations where you need to occasionally execute the command `terragrunt init -reconfigure`.

Why?

- Changing backend configuration (switching types, updating settings) requires reconfiguring.
- Updating provider versions may necessitate reinitialization.
- Upgrading Terraform versions with initialization changes might require reconfiguration.

Running `terraform init -reconfigure` is generally safe when you are mindful of your configuration and backend changes. It does not impact your managed resources; its main goal is to update internal mechanisms for initialization and state management according to your configuration adjustments.

Finalizers

During the provisioning of cloud resources, you might encounter situations where a resource remains undeleted, both within the Kubernetes cluster and in the AWS cloud. This occurrence can be attributed to the presence of `finalizers` – specific conditions that influence the deletion process.

As an example, consider the process of creating an aws-load-balancer-controller in which a service is linked to this controller. In this scenario, the ingress configuration adopts a finalizer condition referred to as `service.kubernetes.io/load-balancer-cleanup`.

These finalizers are used to ensure that specific cleanup actions are performed before a resource is removed from the cluster. In the context of Kubernetes services that are exposing applications externally, this finalizer plays a vital role.

When you expose a Kubernetes service as a LoadBalancer type, a cloud provider's load balancer (e.g., AWS Elastic Load Balancer) is often created to distribute traffic to your service's pods. This external load balancer is managed outside the Kubernetes cluster.

The purpose of the `service.kubernetes.io/load-balancer-cleanup` finalizer is to ensure that before a LoadBalancer service is deleted, the associated external load balancer is properly cleaned up. This includes deregistering the service's endpoints (pod IP addresses) from the load balancer to prevent traffic from being sent to non-existent pods.

Actions that you may need to take

Delete the finalizer from the ingress:

```
kubectl edit ingress -n <Namespace> <ingress_name>
```

Updates the local Kubernetes configuration file:

```
aws eks update-kubeconfig --region us-east-1 --name devops
```

Chapter 2:
Introduction to VPC and Its Key Components

In this chapter, we will delve into the significance of Infrastructure as Code (IaC) and its DevOps tools like Terraform and Terragrunt for automating cloud resource provisioning and management. You will explore strategic infrastructure design and planning, identifying essential resources and modules for launching your infrastructure. The chapter also includes an in-depth examination of Terragrunt's VPC module, followed by practical steps to provision a VPC and an AWS EFS shared volume resource within your infrastructure.

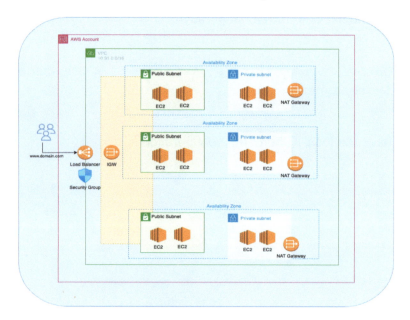

The Importance of Infrastructure as Code

Infrastructure as Code (IaC) refers to the practice of managing and provisioning infrastructure resources. It allows for automating the deployment and management of cloud resources, providing numerous benefits in terms of efficiency, consistency, and scalability.

Terraform and Terragrunt are powerful DevOps tools that facilitate the implementation of IaC. Terraform is an open-source provisioning tool that allows you to define infrastructure resources declaratively, specifying the desired state of your infrastructure using a domain-specific language (DSL). Terragrunt, on the other hand, is a wrapper around Terraform that offers additional functionality for managing Terraform configurations, such as handling remote state, supporting code reuse, and facilitating multi-module deployments.

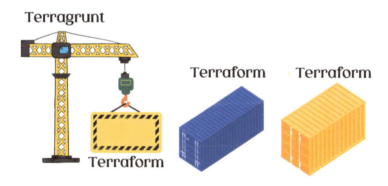

By utilizing Terraform and Terragrunt, you can achieve the following benefits:

	Terragrunt	Terraform

Environment Management	Built-in mechanisms for handling environment-specific variables and configurations	Requires manual configuration changes or external tools to manage environment-specific configurations effectively
Configuration Reusability	Enables code reuse by allowing you to define shared modules and configurations	It requires additional effort to set up and manage shared configurations across projects
Remote State Management	Built-in support for remote state management, making it easier to store and share your infrastructure state across teams and deployments	It does not offer the advanced remote state management capabilities that Terragrunt provides out of the box

To highlight the benefits of Terragrunt over Terraform, consider the following:

Imagine you want to set up an AWS VPC with various components like subnets, security groups, and routing rules using Terraform. While Terraform can achieve this, Terragrunt takes it a step further. Terragrunt not only handles the deployment of the Terraform code but also effectively manages the entire configuration. This ensures consistent control over your system's state and simplifies the creation of modular infrastructure designs.

Strategic Infrastructure Design and Planning

The AWS VPC is a fundamental networking solution within AWS. It acts like a virtual version of traditional data center networks. It operates as the central network for your cloud resources, allowing you to create a customized network environment, set up subnets, manage route tables, and control how different parts of your AWS setup communicate. Moreover, the VPC ensures isolation, improves security, and enables network connectivity for your applications and services. Essentially, it forms the foundation of your entire AWS infrastructure, playing an important role in creating efficient, secure, and organized cloud deployments.

Let us take a look in the following VPC:

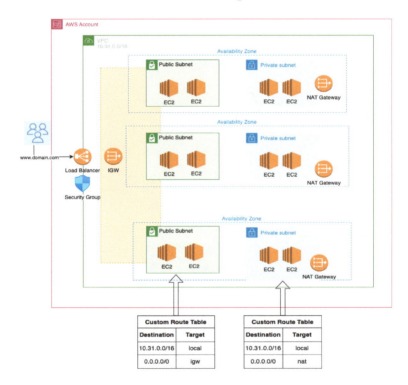

Building a Secure VPC Infrastructure in AWS

Within this framework, instances inside the public subnet wield the capacity to accept incoming traffic, as well as dispatch outbound traffic directly to and from the Internet. Conversely, instances located in the private subnet maintain the capability to access the Internet, albeit primarily for outbound purposes.

This strategic arrangement ensures not only secure communication but also empowers private instances to leverage Internet-based resources tailored to their specific requirements.

An in-depth exploration of the Terragrunt resource: Overview and Deep Dive

Let us examine the structure of our Terragrunt code and understand how the components in our diagram fit together in our Infrastructure setup:

- **Modules:** We will use modules to represent cloud resources that are utilized more than once throughout our configuration.
- **Infra:** Within the infra directory, we will define unique resource specifications for our cloud infrastructure, customizing the modules as needed for each specific use case.

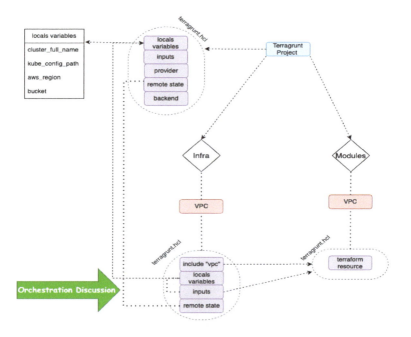

What does our VPC Terragrunt file contain:

- – **Include VPC:** initialize the corresponding module
- – **Locals:** shared environment variables
- – **Input:** required attribute for the AWS module
- – **Remote state:** Terraform state store.

Let us delve into each Terragrunt block, elucidating its purpose and the rationale behind its placement within our Terragrunt repository as we design our infrastructure.

Also, we will take a closer look and explain the parts that are being created in the VPC, like subnets, Internet gateways, NAT gateways, and more.

Include VPC

The "include" block is like a way to share and combine settings in Terragrunt configuration files. It is kind of like taking a parent setup (the included config) and mixing it with your current setup (the child config) before doing anything. Think of it like merging instructions. You can use multiple "include" blocks, but each one needs a special name. It is best practice to always name them.

The provision of the VPC in our Terragrunt code is achieved by utilizing the VPC module specified in the VPC module directory.

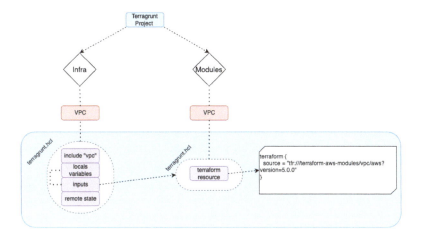

In our implementation, we leverage the VPC module sourced from Terrafrom (Follow-up reference #2).

A snippet to our code:

```
include "vpc" {

  path                                      =
  "${dirname(get_repo_root())}/${basename(get_r
  epo_root())}/modules/vpc/terragrunt.hcl"

}
```

Locals

The "locals" block is like a shortcut creator in Terragrunt. It allows you to give a name to something you will use often. Think of it like a nickname for a longer phrase.

In this "locals" space, there are no set rules for what you can call. You put your attributes in there, and you can then call them with a short name (local.ARG_NAME) anywhere in your Terragrunt setup. It is like having a toolbox of handy terms you have given special names to.

Locals are basically environment variables that we use multiple times in our setup. Instead of repeating ourselves, we gather them in one place. This approach keeps things consistent and makes it easy to reuse these variables for other parts of our cloud setup. It is like having a central hub for things we want to remember and use again.

Here are some of the variables that are included in our setup:

- Cluster name
- AWS region
- CIDR
- Other settings specific to our infrastructure

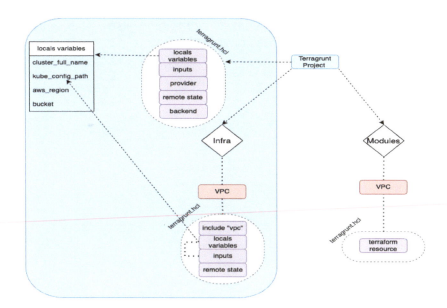

A snippet to our code:

```
locals {

  env_vars                                    =
read_terragrunt_config(get_path_to_repo_root(
))

}
```

Inputs

The "inputs" attribute is like a map that holds input information for Terraform. It is like a cheat sheet that tells Terraform what data to use. Each piece of info in the map becomes an environment variable like a special message.

Just remember, when data moves from Terragrunt to Terraform, it is like crossing a border. It can lose some details like its type. So, in Terraform, you should tell it what kind of info it is getting (like saying if it is a number, a word, or something else). This enables Terraform to manage things correctly.

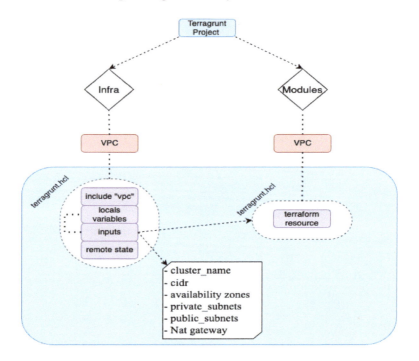

A snippet to our code:

```
inputs = {

  name = local.env_vars.locals.cluster_name

  cidr = local.env_vars.locals.cidr

  ...
```

Remote State

The "remote_state" block in Terragrunt helps set up how your Terraform code will handle remote state, which is like a shared storage for your infrastructure info.

Here is what you need to know:

- **Backend:** This is like choosing where to store your remote state. You pick one of Terraform's supported options.
- **Generate:** This makes Terragrunt create a .tf file that handles remote state. You give it a "path" for where this file should live. If there is already a file present, you can tell Terragrunt what to do – overwrite it, skip the new one, and more.
- **Config:** This is like filling in the blanks. You put stuff here that Terraform needs to know. These details will go into the backend setup, which handles the remote state.

So, think of the "remote_state" block as the master guide for how your code shares and manages info about your setup. It is like setting up a special filing cabinet for your project.

When we are setting up something in the cloud, we need to keep track of what we are doing. But instead of storing this info on our own computer, we put it in a special remote storage. This storage can be cloud storage, like an AWS bucket, or other tools like HashiCorp Consul or Terraform Cloud. It is like using a shared notebook where everyone can write and read what is happening with our cloud stuff. This way, everyone is on the same page!

As you will discover later, we keep the state stored in AWS S3.

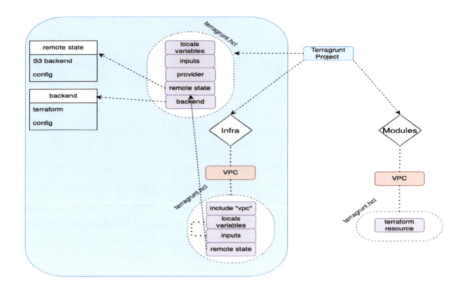

A snippet to our code:

```
remote_state {

  generate = {

    path       = "backend.tf"

    if_exists = "overwrite_terragrunt"

  }

  backend                                    =
local.env_vars.remote_state.backend

  config = merge(

    local.env_vars.remote_state.config,

    {
```

```
      key                                   =
"${local.env_vars.locals.cluster_full_name}/$
{basename(get_repo_root())}/${get_path_from_r
epo_root()}/terraform.tfstate"


    },


  )


}


  generate = local.env_vars.generate
```

Key elements within the VPC that are being set up

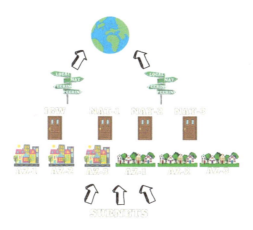

After you create the VPC, these components will also come into play as part of your entire setup.

1. **Private\Public Subnets** – We designate three availability zones for our subnets. This partitioning provides several benefits such as logical addressing, resource isolation, enhanced security, and redundancy.
2. **CIDR block** – This block allows for efficient allocation and management of IP addresses.

3. **IGW (default to true)** – Facilitates bidirectional communication between VPC instances and the internet, essential for public resource interaction.
4. **NAT Gateway** – provides a way for private subnet instances to safely access the internet, like downloading updates or using external services. They act as a secure link between the private subnet and the public internet. This ensures private resources stay hidden while still connecting to what they need.
5. **Route Tables** – It contains a set of rules that determine where network traffic is directed within the VPC. Route tables control the traffic flow between subnets and provide connectivity between different resources. They specify the target for specific IP ranges or destinations, including the internet gateway or NAT gateway.

Bringing It All Together

The components within the VPC work in harmony to establish a secure and isolated network environment for your AWS resources. Subnets play a pivotal role in segmenting and grouping resources, and route tables are responsible for guiding traffic flow between these subnets. Internet Gateways and NAT Gateways enhance internet connectivity for public and private subnets, respectively, while Security Groups safeguard resources from unauthorized access.

The relationship between these elements is structured as follows:

1. **Subnets**: Aligned with specific Availability Zones (AZs) in the VPC, subnets provide a localized context for resources.
2. **Route Tables:** These define the regulations that dictate how traffic is directed among subnets, to and from the internet, and between different subnets.
3. **Security Groups:** Operating at both subnet and instance levels. They make sure network traffic coming in and going out follows strict security rules.

Internet Gateways and NAT Gateways function as pipelines for outgoing traffic from subnets.

Provisioning VPC with Terragrunt

It is recommended that you complete the hands-on exercise in *Chapter 1: Provision a VPC using Cloud9*, where you provision a VPC using Cloud9. This step is essential to ensure you successfully set up your initial VPC.

As you noticed in *Chapter 1: Provision a VPC using Cloud9*, we started the process by executing terragrunt init from the root directory to create the initial backend.tf and provider.tf that are required for the rest of the infrastructure resources.

For our upcoming cloud provisioning, it is necessary to establish a fresh Cloud9 (dev-infra) environment within the newly created VPC. This action aligns with the guidelines outlined in *Chapter 1: Provisioning Resources in a Private Cloud Environment*. This step is important as we now require access to our cluster situated within the private subnet where the VPC is located.

Resource Map After VPC Provisioning

Resource map Info

VPC Show details	Subnets (6)	Route tables (5)	Network connections (4)
Your AWS virtual network	Subnets within this VPC	Route network traffic to resources	Connections to other networks
devops	us-east-1a	devops-private-us-east-1b	devops
	devops-public-us-east-1a	devops-default	devops-us-east-1c
	devops-private-us-east-1a	devops-public	devops-us-east-1a
	us-east-1b	devops-private-us-east-1c	devops-us-east-1b
	devops-public-us-east-1b	devops-private-us-east-1a	
	devops-private-us-east-1b		
	us-east-1c		
	devops-public-us-east-1c		
	devops-private-us-east-1c		

Exploring Storage Options on AWS

AWS provides a range of resources for your infrastructure needs. Today, we are looking at EFS. But before we dig into EFS, let us briefly explore some other volume storage options.

Think of a volume as a basic storage block that holds data. This kind of storage is often used for block storage resources, where you can connect to various AWS tools like Amazon EC2 instances. Volumes let you keep your data safe even when an instance is no longer active, which is super important for storing things like app data and databases.

Here are the primary volume storage options available in AWS:

EBS

EBS presents block storage volumes tailored for attachment to Amazon EC2 instances. It is designed to provide consistent and low-latency performance.

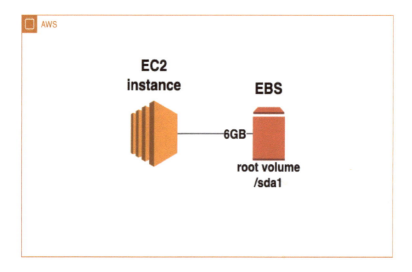

S3

S3 is like a storage service for objects. You can keep all kinds of stuff there – pictures, videos, backups, logs – you name it. While EBS is more about storing data in blocks, S3 works with objects. It is super reliable, scalable, and easy to access. S3 is great for things like random data that does not need to be stored in blocks. And guess what? You can reach it using regular web protocols like HTTP or HTTPS.

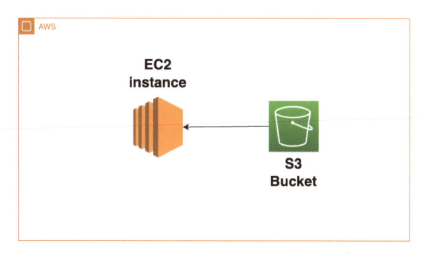

EFS

Setting itself apart from both EBS and S3, Amazon EFS operates as a fully managed file storage service that provides scalable and shared file storage, making it particularly suitable for applications that require multiple instances to share data simultaneously. Unlike EBS volumes, which are attached to a single EC2 instance, EFS can be mounted by multiple instances or containers across different availability zones, enabling collaboration and data sharing.

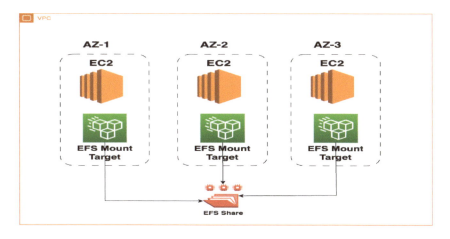

Zoom in to EFS

From a cost perspective, EFS pricing is primarily determined by the storage allocated. While it might not be the most cost-effective choice for workloads with high Input/Output Operations Per Second (IOPS) demands, it excels in cost-effectiveness when catering to shared storage requirements across numerous instances or pods.

In terms of availability, EFS stands out by storing data redundantly across multiple Availability Zones (AZs) within a region. This design helps mitigate the risks associated with a failure in a single AZ, ensuring the resilience and accessibility of your applications.

In our cluster configuration, we wanted to demonstrate the process of establishing an EFS within our infrastructure and subsequently showcase how to attach and use it within our application.

Create your Amazon EFS file system

Login to your workspace

If you do not have a workstation yet, scroll up to *Chapter 1: Provisioning Resources in a Private Cloud Environment* to set up one.

Then, connect to the Cloud9 environment you launched (**dev-infra**).

Let us provision

If this is your first provisioning with the terragrunt project, start by executing `terragrunt init` from the root directory to create the initial backend.tf and provider.tf that are required for the rest of the infrastructure resources.

```
# Access the Terragrunt Repository You
Cloned in Cloud9

cd
~/environment/workstation/terragrunt/infra/02
-efs

terragrunt apply
```

Chapter 3:
Introduction to EKS and Its Key Components

In this chapter, we will begin by introducing Amazon EKS and its main parts. We will explain how Kubernetes works, what a typical app setup looks like, and how users' requests reach your apps. We will also look at auto-scaling for efficiency.

Then, we will explore the Terragrunt EKS setup, how it connects to an existing VPC, and how to create an EKS cluster. We will finish by making sure the cluster is up and running.

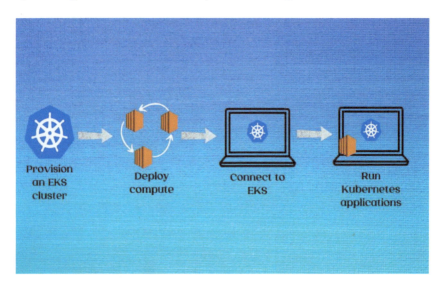

Overview of the EKS and its components

EKS is a managed service that makes it easy to run Kubernetes on AWS without having to manage the underlying infrastructure. It provides a scalable and highly available platform for deploying, managing, and scaling containerized applications using Kubernetes.

By utilizing EKS on AWS, you can offload the management of Kubernetes infrastructure tasks, including server provisioning, patching, and scaling. This enables you to concentrate on the essential aspects of deploying and running your applications without being burdened by the underlying infrastructure responsibilities.

Now, let us visualize the following diagram depicting our EKS module that we are going to provision. Taking a macro perspective, our infrastructure will consist of an EKS cluster and worker nodes, providing the necessary support for running applications and managing the loads within the pods.

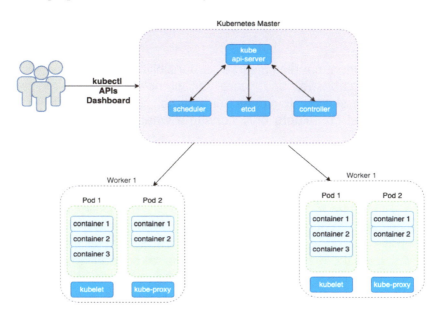

Before we dive into specific scenarios that provide a clearer description of Kubernetes workflows, let us first examine the diagram above. This will help us understand the roles that each Kubernetes component plays in the overall orchestration.

Let us start with the master components that constitute Kubernetes:

kube api-server

This particular component serves as the central control plane element. It exposes the Kubernetes API that empowers users to oversee the entirety of the cluster's resources. In essence, it is the Kubernetes API server that the kubectl tool engages with, enabling users to execute operations on the cluster.

etcd

This component engages in communication with the Kubernetes API server. Its responsibility lies in storing configuration data related to the cluster, basically, it defines how the cluster works. Behind the curtains, every facet of the Kubernetes infrastructure depends on etcd as the definitive source of accurate information.

controller

This component handles diverse responsibilities, supervising VMs, storage, databases, and more, all complexity linked to your Kubernetes cluster. It strives for optimal resource utilization; it ensures that containers only consume what is necessary at the moment.

scheduler

The Scheduler component is responsible for assigning newly created pods to nodes in the cluster. When you create a pod, it does not have a specific node assigned to it. The Scheduler watches for new pods without assigned nodes and makes scheduling decisions based on factors like resource requirements, node affinity, anti-affinity rules, and more. The Scheduler communicates with the API server to obtain information about available nodes and pods and makes intelligent decisions about where to place the pods to ensure efficient resource utilization.

Let us take a moment to review the table provided. This table will serve as a reference for your Kubernetes cluster.

	Component	Role	Description
Control Plane Components	**kube-apiserver**	API Management	Front-end for the control plane
	etcd	Data Storage	Stores all cluster data
	kube-scheduler	Workload Allocation	Decides where to run unscheduled Pods
	kube-controller-manager	State Monitoring & Recovery	Ensures the actual state matches the desired state
	cloud-controller-manager	Cloud Interaction	Manages interaction between cluster and underlying cloud provider
Worker Node Components	**kubelet**	Node Management	Ensures containers are running in a Pod
	kube-proxy	Network Proxy	Maintains network rules on nodes
	Container runtime	Container Execution	Runs containers
Add-on	**CNI Plugin**	Network Management	Provides container

Components			networking
	CoreDNS	Service Discovery	Acts as the DNS server within the cluster
	Metrics Server	Performance Monitoring	Collects and stores resource usage data
	Web UI	User Interface	Provides a web-based interface for managing the cluster

As we move forward with our practical steps, we will install the metrics server add-on component. This component will allow us to collect cluster metrics. It will enhance our ability to monitor and understand its performance.

Important Note

It's important to note that any potential performance concerns within your application could be tied to the cluster's components. If such situations arise, referring to the documentation of these components will be necessary for conducting analysis and effective troubleshooting.

Illustrating a Kubernetes Application in Action

Pod

Imagine your application as a bustling city, where every corner has a role to play. At the heart of this city are pods, like individual homes where specific tasks reside. These pods work closely together, much like neighbors collaborating on projects. However, homes can be replaced or renovated without disrupting the neighborhood's essence.

Deployment

Then we have deployments, which are the architects of consistency. They ensure that the right number of pods, representing your application's workforce, are always available. Deployments supervise the neighborhood, making sure the workforce thrives and grows to meet demands. If a house needs a fresh coat of paint, deployments handle it smoothly without disturbing the entire community.

Service

Now, imagine the bustling city needs pathways to connect its various parts. This is where services come into play. They act as magical bridges connecting pods and their homes, ensuring communication flows effortlessly. Just as streets direct people to their destinations, services guide data to the right pods, fostering harmony.

Ingress

But our city wants to interact with the world beyond its borders. Here comes the ingress, the grand gateway to the city. Ingress welcomes visitors, routing them through well-defined lanes to different neighborhoods (services). It even ensures security, managing who gets in and protecting the city's treasures.

So, you see, within the Kubernetes city, pods are the homes of tasks, deployments supervise consistency, services link everything together, and Ingress welcomes visitors. It is a symphony of cooperation, where each layer builds upon the other, creating a reliable, scalable, and accessible ecosystem for your application to thrive.

As the city grows, with pods buzzing, deployments evolving, services connecting, and ingress expanding its horizons, your application flourishes within the Kubernetes metropolis, standing as a testament to the power of orchestrated teamwork.

Navigating User Requests to Pods

Let us visualize the following scenario

A user's request enters and navigates through our Kubernetes cluster, with a specific focus on receiving a response from one of our deployed services.

Request Flow:

- User A sends a request to the load balancer's IP address: port.
- The load balancer forwards the request to a node within the cluster.
- The node passes the request to the kube-proxy, which identifies the associated service based on the virtual IP (VIP) and port.
- The kube-proxy routes the request to one of the endpoints (pods) of the service, considering numerous factors such as readiness, resource usage, and network latency.
- The pod receives the request and transfers it to the container for processing.

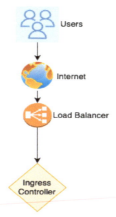

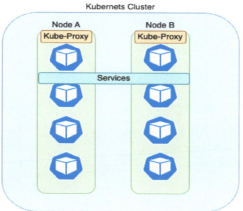

Response Flow:

- The container generates the response and sends it to the pod's IP address and the service's port.
- The pod passes the response to the kube-proxy's IP address and port.
- The kube-proxy forwards the response to the service's ClusterIP and port.
- The response then travels to the node, the ingress controller, and finally to the load balancer.
- The load balancer delivers the response to User A's IP address and port, completing the request-response cycle.

Think of it like this:

When you ask for something in the cluster, your request goes through different points, kind of like stations, until it reaches the right place. Then, when that place has an answer, it goes back through these stations to get to you. It is like a round trip for information in the cluster!

HPA in Kubernetes

In Kubernetes, the HorizontalPodAutoscaler (HPA) dynamically adjusts the number of pods in a workload (like a Deployment or StatefulSet) to meet changing demand automatically. This type of scaling adds more pods when the load increases and scales down when the load decreases, ensuring efficient resource utilization.

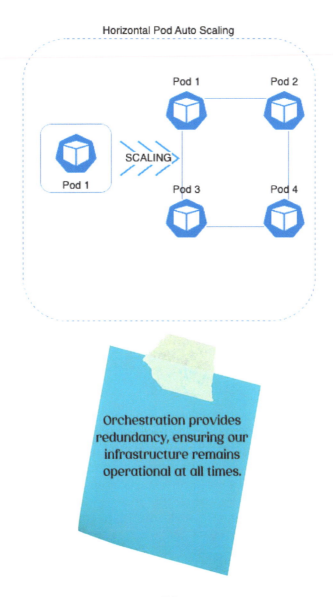

Orchestration provides redundancy, ensuring our infrastructure remains operational at all times.

Here is how it works

The key components responsible for HPA are the HPA controller and the metrics server. The HPA controller watches your pods and looks at metrics like CPU usage or custom metrics you set. When these metrics show that your pods are busy, the HPA controller creates more pods to handle the load.

On the other hand, if the metrics show that your pods are chilling', the HPA controller scales down the number of pods to save resources. This dynamic scaling helps keep your app responsive and efficient. It is like having an automatic assistant that adds or removes staff from your team based on how much work there is. All of this makes sure your app is running smoothly without overloading your system.

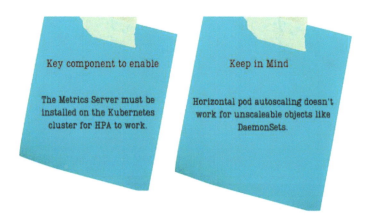

Key component to enable

The Metrics Server must be installed on the Kubernetes cluster for HPA to work.

Keep in Mind

Horizontal pod autoscaling doesn't work for unscaleable objects like DaemonSets.

As described in the diagram below, the control plane components play a pivotal role in the operation of the Kubernetes cluster. Consequently, any failure in the control plane node could lead to various issues. Hence, adding redundancy to the control plane is highly considered. For enterprises utilizing stacked clusters, a minimum of three redundant nodes (in three availability zones) is advised to ensure optimal reliability and fault tolerance.

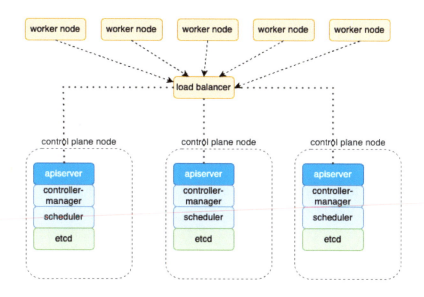

EKS : Terragrunt Module and Dependency Relationships

The Terragrunt-based EKS structure will follow the same approach as our VPC setup. It will consist of two main components:

- Modules, which represent the cloud resources.
- Infra, where we define the specifications for each unique resource.

Referring to the provided orchestration map, our primary focus for the discussion will be on EKS:

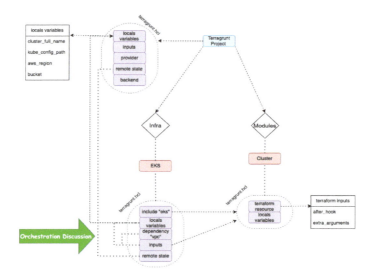

What does our EKS Terragrunt file contain:

- – Include VPC: initialize the corresponding module
- – Locals: shared environment variables
- – Dependency VPC: used to configure module dependencies
- – Input: required attribute for the AWS module
- – Remote state: Terraform state store.

We previously covered the Terragrunt blocks and attributes, such as include, locals, input, and remote state, during our discussion about VPC in the *"An In-Depth Exploration of the Terragrunt Resource - Overview and Deep Dive"* episode. The code we are providing for EKS follows the same principles that were discussed in the VPC. However, there is a new block introduced here that was not mentioned during VPC provisioning, which is the "dependency" block.

Let us delve into its purpose and role in the context of EKS provisioning.

Dependency VPC

Imagine you are building a complex structure with building blocks. The "dependency" block is like a special connection between blocks. It lets one block share its features with another block, making them work together. Just like how a car block might connect to a block with wheels.

In our scenario, these "dependency" blocks help modules in Terraform share information. It is like a bridge that allows one module to use the results of another module. You can even have multiple "dependency" blocks, each linking different modules like a network of connected building blocks.

The following diagram shows the Terragrunt repository structure of the dependency within the context of EKS (Elastic Kubernetes Service):

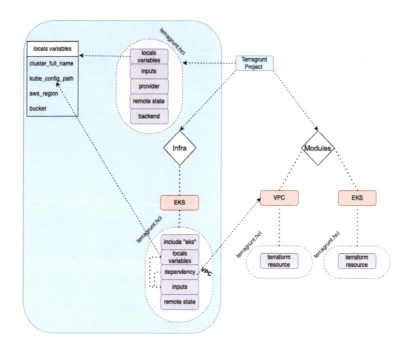

A snippet to our code:

```
dependency "vpc" {

  config_path  =  find_in_parent_folders("01-
  vpc")

}
```

In the above code block, you can see that we define a "dependency" block of VPC. This is because, when setting up the EKS, specific details are needed – like the VPC ID and subnet IDs – to determine where the EKS cluster should be created.

Since we have already set up the VPC using Terragrunt and have access to its output information, we can use the "dependency" block to create consistency and avoid using hard-coded values. Hard-coding values can lead to an unwieldy Terragrunt structure that is difficult to maintain. This is why we have designed our Terragrunt project repository using a modular approach with separate sections for modules, infrastructure, and services. This way, we can encapsulate the logic and ensure a maintainable setup.

Include EKS

The behavior of the "include" block is consistent with what we discussed in the *"An In-Depth Exploration of the Terragrunt Resource - Overview and Deep Dive"* episode. However, upon inspecting the EKS module, we will discover an additional Terragrunt feature known as the "After Hook".

After Hook is a Terragrunt feature that enables you to define custom actions to be executed after running a Terraform command.

The diagram below shows the Terragrunt repository structure associated with Amazon EKS in relation to the After Hook script:

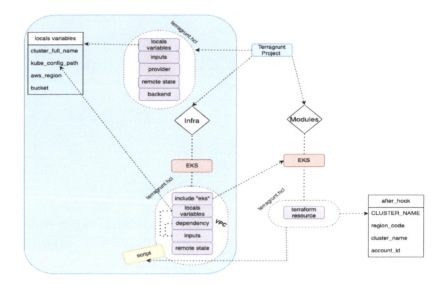

In our implementation, we leverage the EKS module sourced (Follow-up reference #3) from Terraform.

A snippet to our code:

```
terraform {

  source          =          "tfr:///terraform-aws-
modules/eks/aws?version=19.14.0"

  after_hook "terragrunt-read-config" {

    commands = ["apply"]

    execute                  =                  ["bash",
"./update_kubeconfig.sh"]

  }

  extra_arguments "set_env" {
```

```
commands = ["apply"]

env_vars = {

    CLUSTER_NAME                                =
local.env_vars.locals.cluster_full_name

    region_code                                 =
local.env_vars.locals.aws_region

    cluster_name                                =
local.env_vars.locals.cluster_name

    account_id                                  =
local.env_vars.locals.account_id

  }

 }

}


locals {

  env_vars                                      =
read_terragrunt_config(get_path_to_repo_root(
))

}
```

In the above code block, we set the environment variables that are intended to be accessible in our script. The script's function is to generate our kubeconfig, a configuration file that stores the cluster authentication information for the kubectl (Follow-up reference #4).

Provisioning EKS with Terragrunt

Login to your workspace

If you do not have a workstation yet, scroll up to *Chapter 1: Provisioning Resources in a Private Cloud Environment* in order to set up one.

Then, connect to the Cloud9 environment you launched (**dev-infra**).

Let us provision

If this is your first provisioning with the terragrunt project, start by executing `terragrunt init` from the root directory to create the initial backend.tf and provider.tf that are required for the rest of the infrastructure resources.

```
cd
~/environment/workstation/terragrunt/infra/03
-eks

terragrunt apply
```

Ensure that the additional security group that is linked to your EKS cluster includes a rule with your CIDR, granting access to All Traffic. This CIDR was added during the EKS provisioning process.

```
cluster_security_group_additional_rules = {

    ingress_cluster_to_node_all_traffic = {

        description = "Internal VPC Access"
```

```
    protocol = "-1"

    from_port = 0

    to_port = 0

    type = "ingress"

    cidr_blocks                                =
[local.env_vars.locals.cidr]

  }

}
```

If this configuration is missing, kindly refer back to the instructions outlined in Chapter 1: Provisioning Resources in a Private Cloud Environment / Allow Access to EKS for the CIDR.

1. Verify that the after_hook was executed. You should now have the cluster authority, which you can confirm by running the command ls -al ~/.kube/config.

Check the cluster status

If you have not set up a workstation yet, refer back to *Chapter 1: Provisioning Resources in a Private Cloud Environment* in order to perform deployment commands on your EKS cluster.

1. Connect to your Cloud9.
2. Check the Kubernetes cluster health:

```
export KUBECONFIG=~/.kube/config

curl -k $(cat $KUBECONFIG | grep -m 1 'server' | sed -n 's/server://p' | tr -d ' ')/livez\?verbose
```

3. You should expect to see the following result:

```
z\?verbose

[+]ping ok

[+]log ok

[+]etcd ok

[+]kms-provider-0 ok

[+]poststarthook/start-kube-apiserver-admission-initializer ok

[+]poststarthook/generic-apiserver-start-informers ok
```

70

```
[+]poststarthook/priority-and-fairness-
config-consumer ok

[+]poststarthook/priority-and-fairness-filter
ok

[+]poststarthook/storage-object-count-
tracker-hook ok

[+]poststarthook/start-apiextensions-
informers ok

[+]poststarthook/start-apiextensions-
controllers ok

[+]poststarthook/crd-informer-synced ok

[+]poststarthook/start-system-namespaces-
controller ok

[+]poststarthook/bootstrap-controller ok

[+]poststarthook/rbac/bootstrap-roles ok

[+]poststarthook/scheduling/bootstrap-system-
priority-classes ok

[+]poststarthook/priority-and-fairness-
config-producer ok

[+]poststarthook/start-cluster-
authentication-info-controller ok

[+]poststarthook/start-kube-apiserver-
identity-lease-controller ok
```

```
[+]poststarthook/start-deprecated-kube-
apiserver-identity-lease-garbage-collector ok

[+]poststarthook/start-kube-apiserver-
identity-lease-garbage-collector ok

[+]poststarthook/start-legacy-token-tracking-
controller ok

[+]poststarthook/aggregator-reload-proxy-
client-cert ok

[+]poststarthook/start-kube-aggregator-
informers ok

[+]poststarthook/apiservice-registration-
controller ok

[+]poststarthook/apiservice-status-available-
controller ok

[+]poststarthook/kube-apiserver-
autoregistration ok

[+]autoregister-completion ok

[+]poststarthook/apiservice-openapi-
controller ok

[+]poststarthook/apiservice-openapiv3-
controller ok

[+]poststarthook/apiservice-discovery-
controller ok

livez check passed
```

Chapter 4:
Provision a Production-Ready EKS

In this chapter, we will kick off with the setup of a node group in our EKS cluster, paving the way for Kubernetes service execution. Following that, we will step into the installation of the metric server, enhancing our grasp of cluster performance. From there, we will dive into the NLB's advantages, distinguishing it from other load balancers, and eventually deploying one. We will finish by creating a self-signed certificate for SSL termination within the realm of nginx.

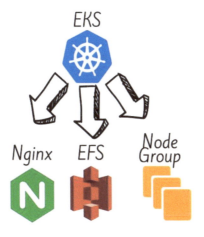

Introduction to the Node Group and its Terragrunt Configuration

Up to this point, we have successfully initiated a VPC that establishes the foundational infrastructure blueprint for orchestrating our EKS cluster. With this framework in place, we will proceed to create a node group and integrate it into our EKS cluster configuration.

Our EKS node group serves as a pivotal component in the cluster. It functions as the backbone of your infrastructure.

At the core of an EKS node group lies the dynamic provisioning of Amazon EC2 instances. These instances are managed via Amazon EC2 Auto Scaling groups, eliminating the manual overhead of managing individual instances. This automation ensures the right number of instances are maintained, scaled, and aligned with your application's demands.

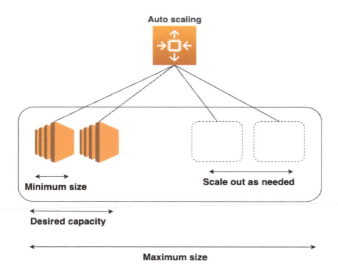

Behind each EC2 instance is a launch configuration, which acts as a blueprint for creating instances. This includes details like instance type, disk size, security groups, and more.

A snippet to our code:

```
inputs = {

  name          = "internal-services"

  cluster_name                        =
  local.env_vars.locals.cluster_name


  desired_size = 1

  max_size      = 3

  min_size      = 1
```

```
instance_types          = ["t3.large"]

capacity_type           = "SPOT"

create_security_group = false



cluster_primary_security_group_id            =
dependency.eks.outputs.cluster_primary_securi
ty_group_id

cluster_security_group_id                    =
dependency.eks.outputs.cluster_security_group
_id

node_role_arn                                =
dependency.eks.outputs.cluster_iam_role_arn

subnet_ids                                   =
dependency.vpc.outputs.private_subnets

cluster_endpoint                             =
dependency.eks.outputs.cluster_endpoint

cluster_auth_base64                          =
dependency.eks.outputs.cluster_certificate_au
thority_data

iam_role_additional_policies                 =
[dependency.efs.outputs.aws_iam_policy_arn]

}
```

Our provisioning setup declares the following:

- **Node Group Name:** The unique identifier for the node group.
- **Cluster Name Assignment:** The cluster linked with the node group.
- **Node Group Size Configuration:** Set the desired capacity, along with minimum and maximum instances for the node group.
- **Instance Type:** Opt for a t3.large instance, with a specific emphasis on launching it as a spot instance.
- **Security Group:** Attach the identical security groups established for the EKS setup.
- **IAM Role:** The ARN of the roles created for EKS.
- **Subnet:** The VPC within which the node group will be deployed.
- **Cluster Endpoint:** The API server endpoint for communication between kubelet, kubectl, and the Kubernetes API server.
- **Cluster Authentication Base64:** Encode the certificate data in Base64, vital for secure communication with the cluster.
- **Additional IAM Role Policies:** Additional IAM roles, tailored to our preconfigured EFS, to extend functionality.

A closer look at the subnets that we allocated to the Node Group

Node groups are designed for high availability and fault tolerance. Instances within a node group are distributed across multiple Availability Zones (AZs), safeguarding your applications against AZ-level failures. In the event of an instance failure, Amazon EC2 Auto Scaling replaces the instance automatically, maintaining the desired capacity and performance.

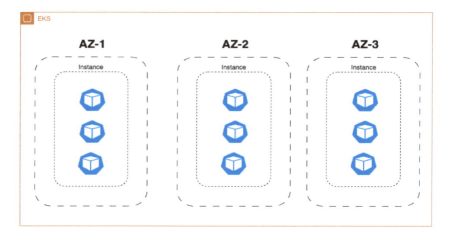

In our workshop, we set up a VPC with the designated CIDR of 10.106.0.0/16, and within this setup, we established both private and public subnets:

- **Private subnet:** ["10.106.1.0/24", "10.106.2.0/24", "10.106.3.0/24"]
- **Public subnet:** ["10.106.101.0/24", "10.106.102.0/24", "10.106.103.0/24"]

distributed subnets

We assigned the private subnets to our node group. We prefer using private subnets over using public subnets due to security and control considerations. Private subnets are isolated from the internet, which significantly enhances the security posture of your node instances by reducing their exposure to potential threats. By deploying node instances in private subnets, you have greater control over inbound and outbound traffic flow, as well as finer-grained access control using network security groups or firewalls.

Private Subnets

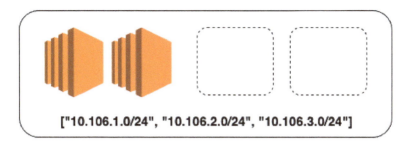

["10.106.1.0/24", "10.106.2.0/24", "10.106.3.0/24"]

This approach follows the principle of the least privilege, where resources are only accessible by those entities that explicitly need access. It is a recommended practice for securing infrastructure components like node instances. On the other hand, attaching node instances to public subnets could inadvertently expose them to unnecessary external access, potentially increasing the attack surface and security risks.

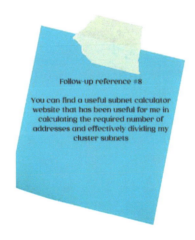

Follow-up reference #8

You can find a useful subnet calculator website that has been useful for me in calculating the required number of addresses and effectively dividing my cluster subnets

Node Group Provisioning

Login to your workspace

If you do not have a workstation yet, scroll up to *Chapter 1: Provisioning Resources in a Private Cloud Environment* in order to set up one.

Then, connect to the Cloud9 environment you launched (**dev-infra**).

Let us provision

If this is your first provisioning with the terragrunt project, start by executing `terragrunt init` from the root directory to create the initial backend.tf and provider.tf that are required for the rest of the infrastructure resources.

```
cd
~/environment/workstation/terragrunt/infra/04
-nodeGroups/managed-node-group/internal-
services

terragrunt apply
```

Let us sum it up

Once the node group is provisioned, it integrates with your EKS cluster. It becomes an integral part of your cluster's compute capacity, ready to run your containerized applications. This integration eliminates the complexities of managing compute resources independently and ensures a cohesive environment for your Kubernetes workloads.

You can now view the creation of your new autoscaling group in the AWS console (Follow-up reference #5)

Verify Node Assignment in the EKS Cluster

1. If you do not have a workstation yet, scroll up to *Chapter 1: Provisioning Resources in a Private Cloud Environment* in order to set up one.
2. Execute the following command in the Cloud9 CLI:

```
kubectl get nodes
```

Provisioning Metric Server

Once our operational Amazon EKS cluster is up and running smoothly, let us enhance its observability by integrating the Metrics Server, which will provide us comprehensive insights into the performance metrics of both the cluster's components and the applications we intend to deploy in the future.

Furthermore, the Metrics Server plays an additional role in our orchestration, serving as a component for other Kubernetes add-ons like the Horizontal Pod Autoscaler and the Kubernetes Dashboard.

This diagram illustrates how the Metrics Server gathers CPU and memory usage data from application workloads that are running on worker nodes. These metrics are then made available via the Kubernetes API server, enabling you to keep track of resource utilization.

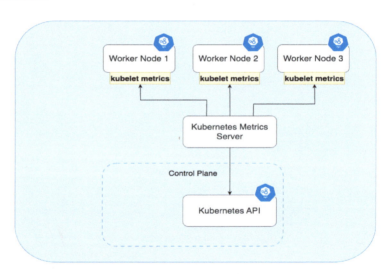

Login to your workspace

If you do not have a workstation yet, scroll up to *Chapter 1: Provisioning Resources in a Private Cloud Environment* in order to set up one.

Then, connect to the Cloud9 environment you launched (**dev-infra**).

Let us provision the Metric Server

If this is your first provisioning with the terragrunt project, start by executing `terragrunt init` from the root directory to create the initial backend.tf and provider.tf that are required for the rest of the infrastructure resources.

```
cd
~/environment/workstation/terragrunt/infra
/05-metrics-server

terragrunt apply
```

Provisioning a Network Load Balancer with the NGINX Ingress Controller

Imagine the AWS Network Load Balancer as a traffic conductor situated at the heart of your system. It operates on the fourth layer of the OSI model, which is like the data highway, making sure everything flows smoothly. This Load Balancer can effortlessly handle an enormous number of requests, even millions per second.

When someone sends a connection request, the load balancer jumps into action. It picks a suitable target from a designated group using a predefined rule. Then, it sets up a connection, much like a virtual bridge, to the chosen target. Think of it as ensuring that all your visitors find the fastest route to their destination on your website, keeping their experience smooth.

Making Your App Accessible in Kubernetes with Ingress

When it comes to Kubernetes, there are various methods to make your application accessible to users. One smart approach is using ingress to achieve this. Ingress is not exactly a service type itself, but rather, it is like the front door to your cluster. It is the point where users enter. Ingress lets you simplify your routing rules into a single setup. This means you can expose multiple services under just one IP address, streamlining how users reach your applications.

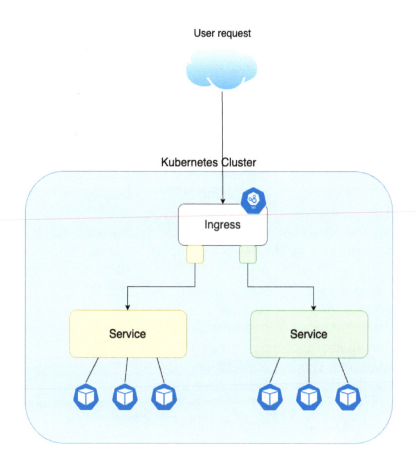

Choose Your Load Balancer

When making your choice, remember to align it with your application's specific needs. Here is a quick rundown:

NLB	ALB	CLB
If you are dealing with TCP traffic, NLB is your go-to. It has the ability to handle enormous request loads with minimal delays. It is perfect for unpredictable traffic spikes and maintains a single static IP address for each Availability Zone.	If you are navigating HTTP and HTTPS traffic complexities, ALB has your back. It offers sophisticated routing capabilities that suit modern application setups like microservices and container-based systems.	If your application originates from the EC2-Classic network era, the Classic Load Balancer is your match.

Login to your workspace

If you do not have a workstation yet, scroll up to *Chapter 1: Provisioning Resources in a Private Cloud Environment* in order to set up one.

Then, connect to the Cloud9 environment you launched (**dev-infra**).

Let us provision the NLB

If this is your first provisioning with the terragrunt project, start by executing `terragrunt init` from the root directory to create the initial backend.tf and provider.tf that are required for the rest of the infrastructure resources.

```
cd
~/environment/workstation/terragrunt/servi
ces/ingress-nginx

terragrunt apply
```

After the provisioning process is complete, you can verify the NLB's creation in your AWS console by navigating to the load balancer section.

Domain Certificate: Creating a self-signed certificate for SSL Termination

This topic may not be relevant for those who haven't obtained a domain name. Feel free to proceed to the next one.

FYI

Choosing to finish the self-signed certificate section for your domain will not align with the setup outlined in the book that involves the NLB and applications using ingress. Since we assume you have not acquired a domain, we will explain accessing various applications within the same Load Balancer. This is because we did not cover examples involving a domain specified in the ingress.

To learn how to use a self-signed certificate with your Load Balancer, follow us on social media.

Let us give it a try

If you have set up a unique domain for your server, you can utilize its certificate. If not, you can still employ SSL using a self-signed certificate for development and testing purposes, like a virtual ID.

In this case, as we are creating SSL on the backend, we will generate a self-signed certificate.

It is like creating your own exclusive key to unlock a secure digital pathway.

Login to your workspace

If you do not have a workstation yet, scroll up to *Chapter 1: Provisioning Resources in a Private Cloud Environment* in order to set up one.

Then, connect to the Cloud9 environment you launched (**dev-infra**).

Let us create a self-signed certificate and private key:

```
export YOUR_DOMAIN_NAME="Your custom domain
name that you've purchased"
```

```
openssl req -x509 -nodes -days 365 -newkey
rsa:2048 -keyout tls.key -out tls.crt -subj
"/CN=$YOUR_DOMAIN_NAME/O=$YOUR_DOMAIN_NAME"
```

Once you have generated your custom certificate for the workshop, the next step involves confirming its validity and then applying it to your Kubernetes cluster.

At first, let us verify the certificate:

```
openssl x509 -in tls.crt -text -noout
```

You will notice it includes your domain name and the certificate's expiration date.

Generate the secret in the cluster

1. If you do not have a workstation yet, scroll up to *Chapter 1: Provisioning Resources in a Private Cloud Environment* in order to set up one.

2. Connect to the Cloud9 environment you launched.
3. Create the following secret in the cluster:

```
kubectl create secret -n default tls tls-secret
--key tls.key --cert tls.crt
```

Provisioning a Kubernetes Dashboard

The Kubernetes Dashboard serves as a versatile web-based interface for Kubernetes clusters. It empowers users to manage applications within the cluster, troubleshoot issues, and efficiently manage both the applications and the cluster itself.

Think of the Kubernetes Dashboard as your initial tool toward getting production-ready. It enables you to quickly evaluate your cluster's performance, all thanks to the metric server we configured earlier. The metric server that we set up earlier is sharing the cluster metrics, which you can then view as informative graphs.

Basically, the Kubernetes Dashboard stands as a secure way for providing your R&D developers access to monitor their applications and access real-time logs and to get a visibility of their application.

Zoom in to the Kubernetes Dashboard configuration:

Since we do not have our own domain name, we will access our application via a single Load Balancer. However, we will route each service to a distinct endpoint, allowing us to host multiple applications under a single Load Balancer.

In order to do that we will add annotations to our Kubernetes Dashboard ingress (Follow-up reference #9):

```yaml
ingress:

  annotations:

    . . . . .

    nginx.ingress.kubernetes.io/rewrite-
target: /$2

nginx.ingress.kubernetes.io/configuration-
snippet: |

      rewrite ^(/dashboard)$ $1/ redirect;

  . . . .

  . . . .

  customPaths:

    - backend:

        service:

          name: kubernetes-dashboard

          port:

            number: 443

      path: /dashboard(/|$)(.*)

      pathType: Prefix
```

Rewrite-target

The first annotation is used to rewrite the path of incoming requests before they are sent to the backend service. In this case, the annotation is set to "/$2". What this does is that it takes the original request path and replaces it with the second part of the URL path, which is typically the path matched by the ingress rule's path regex. This is useful when you want to extract a specific portion of the URL and pass it to the backend service.

Configuration-snippet

The second annotation allows you to inject custom Nginx configuration snippets. In the provided snippet, the "rewrite" directive is used to alter the URL path. Specifically, it captures requests to "/dashboard" and redirects them to "/dashboard/". This is helpful for ensuring consistent URL formatting and handling.

Login to your workspace

If you do not have a workstation yet, scroll up to *Chapter 1: Provisioning Resources in a Private Cloud Environment* in order to set up one.

Then, connect to the Cloud9 environment you launched (**dev-infra**).

Let us provision the Kubernetes Dashboard

If this is your first provisioning with the terragrunt project, start by executing `terragrunt init` from the root directory to create the initial backend.tf and provider.tf that are required for the rest of the infrastructure resources.

```
# Access the Terragrunt Repository You
Cloned in Cloud9
```

```
cd
~/environment/workstation/terragrunt/servi
ces/kubernetes-dashboard

terragrunt apply
```

Export the DNS of the preexisting Load Balancer

```
export LB=$(aws elbv2 describe-load-balancers
--query  "LoadBalancers[0].DNSName"  --output
text)
```

Access to the Kubernetes Dashboard by typing: open $LB/dashboard

Press skip to login to the Kubernetes Dashboard

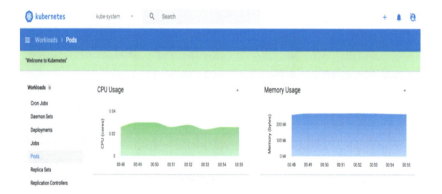

Chapter 5:
Docker Image Strategies and Containerized App Development

In this chapter, we will step into the creation of a containerized application using Dockerfile and we will explore both strategies: single-stage and multi-stage. Our main goal is to highlight the importance of infrastructure choices in the design of our orchestration.

Moreover, as part of this session, I will provide a comprehensive insight into the Docker cache mechanism and the benefits of .dockerignore and its added advantage in optimizing our Docker images (Follow-up reference #6).

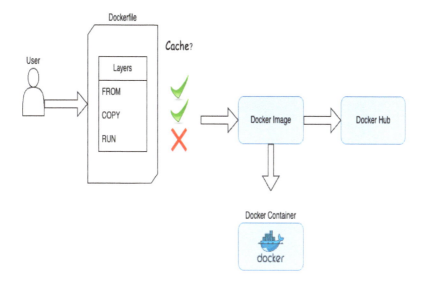

The Significance of Effective build in DevOps

Think of building a toy robot as creating a Docker container for your application. In a single-stage approach, you gather all the robot's parts, tools, and paints into one big box – this is like packaging your app, build tools, and dependencies into a single Docker image. It is easy because everything is in one place, but the box becomes large and heavy due to all the tools you added in it.

On the other hand, a multi-stage approach involves using separate boxes for different purposes. Imagine assembling the robot with just the necessary tools and materials in a compact toolbox. Once the robot is complete, you move it to a display case designed specifically for showcasing the finished product. In Docker, this means using different Docker images for building and running your app. You create a smaller "toolbox" image for the build process, containing only the necessary tools, and then transfer your finished app to a "display case" image containing just what is needed to run it. This results in a cleaner, lighter, and more efficient final container, like presenting the robot without the extra tools in the display case.

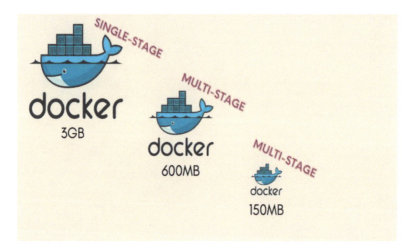

In both scenarios, developers initiate the process by designing a Dockerfile. Subsequently, they proceed to the Docker build phase, where the application and its dependencies are encapsulated. However, in the multistage approach, the last stage includes only the essential things we made during the initial stages.

Docker Build Approaches

The single-stage approach involves a straightforward build process, while the multi-stage approach optimizes the image by dividing the build process into multiple stages within the Dockerfile.

The multi-stage approach offers several benefits, including reduced image size by excluding unnecessary dependencies, enhanced security by minimizing the attack surface, faster builds through the utilization of cached intermediate stages, and improved control and resource allocation for better efficiency.

A diagram illustrating how our Dockerfile looks from the perspective of a local developer

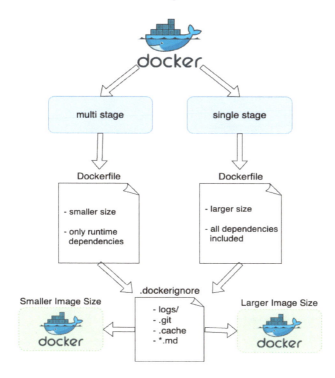

Key aspects while building a containerized application

Let us learn about .dockerignore files and their role in simplifying image sizes for rapid deployment and heightened data security. We will delve into the intricacies of building single and multi-stage images, examining their layers. Furthermore, we will learn how cache management influences performance optimization within Docker build processes.

Why should you care to have a .dockerignore file?

Docker image size

Smaller image sizes enable faster deployments to multiple servers and support local development.

Unintended secrets exposure

Uncontrolled build context can lead to unintentional exposure of sensitive information, such as source code, commit history, and credentials. Properly managing the Docker build context and using .dockerignore to exclude sensitive files mitigates the risk of security breaches.

Cache deliberation

Injecting the entire codebase into an image and mismanaging the build context can cause frequent cache invalidation, slowing down the build process. Therefore, we would like to improve the build performance by using cache which will optimize the build context and improve build performance.

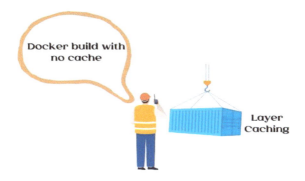

Overview of the Docker Image single-stage

As a developer, we are required to test and demonstrate our code in a local environment. This is where Docker comes in handy, enabling us to build a containerized image to perform initial testing. By containerizing our code, we gain the ability to thoroughly test and validate our application before deploying it to various environments.

In this example, we are building a web application project with the following structure. However, you can access the complete code in the provided repository (Follow-up reference #6), while our focus here will be on the layers of the Dockerfile:

- src/

  - main/

    - ……./HelloWorldApplication.java

  - test/

    - ……./HelloWorldApplication.java

- Dockerfile.single-stage

- Dockerfile.multi-stage

- .dockerignore

A single-stage Dockerfile

```
FROM maven:3.8.3-openjdk-17-slim AS build

WORKDIR /app
```

```
COPY . /app

RUN mvn clean package

RUN    mv    ./target/demo-0.0.1-SNAPSHOT.jar
./demo-0.0.1-SNAPSHOT.jar

EXPOSE 8080

ENTRYPOINT  ["java",  "-jar","./demo-0.0.1-
SNAPSHOT.jar"]
```

The Dockerfile layers:

- **FROM** – specifies a base image
- **WORKDIR** – sets the working directory
- **COPY** – copies the source code
- **RUN** – installs our application
- **RUN** – copies the application code to our workdir
- **EXPOSE** – exposes a port to our application
- **ENTRYPOINT** – specifies the command to run when the container starts

Overview of the Docker Image multi-stage

With the multi-stage approach, we optimize image size and performance during the build process by dividing it into multiple stages.

A multi-stage Dockerfile

```
# Stage 1: Build the application

FROM maven:3.8.3-openjdk-17 AS build

WORKDIR /app

COPY pom.xml /app/

RUN mvn validate

COPY . /app

RUN mvn package

RUN mv ./target/demo-0.0.1-SNAPSHOT.jar ./demo-0.0.1-SNAPSHOT.jar



# Stage 2: Create the final image

FROM openjdk:17.0.1-jdk-slim-buster

COPY --from=build /app/demo-0.0.1-SNAPSHOT.jar /demo-0.0.1-SNAPSHOT.jar

EXPOSE 8080
```

```
ENTRYPOINT    ["java",    "-jar",". /demo-0.0.1-
SNAPSHOT.jar"]
```

The Dockerfile layers:

What comes into play at this point is the second stage within the Dockerfile:

- FROM - Specifies a more lightweight image as opposed to the one that we created while building the artifact
- COPY - Copies the prebuilt artifact from the first stage
- EXPOSE – exposes a port to our application
- ENTRYPOINT – specifies the command to run when the container starts

Sum It Up

The Dockerfile now includes two stages: a builder stage and a final image stage. In the builder stage, the necessary dependencies and the application code are copied to the image. In the final image stage, only the required files from the builder stage are copied to keep the image size optimized.

Overview of the Docker Ignore file

The .dockerignore file plays a key role in Docker's workflow. Prior to transmitting the context to the docker daemon, the Docker CLI seeks out a file named .dockerignore in the root directory of the context. When present, this file instructs the CLI to modify the context by excluding files and directories that match patterns in it. This preventive measure avoids the unnecessary transfer of large or sensitive files to the daemon, which could inadvertently be included in images through ADD or COPY commands.

The format of the .dockerignore file involves a list of patterns, with each pattern separated by a new line.

Here is an illustrative example of a .dockerignore file:

```
.dockerignore

.git

*.log
```

Optimizing Builds with Efficient Cache Management

you will often find yourself repeatedly reconstructing the same Docker image, whether it is for software updates or local development. As building images is a frequent process, Docker offers various techniques to accelerate this task. Among them, Docker's build cache is your way to go for boosting build speeds.

How does the build cache mechanism work?

By understanding Docker's build cache mechanism, you can optimize your Dockerfiles to achieve quicker build.

In Dockerfile, each instruction corresponds to a distinct layer within the final image. Visualize image layers as a stack, where each layer builds upon the content of the previous ones.

Docker Layers

Whenever a layer encounters modifications, it requires a rebuild. For instance, if you modify the pom.xml file in your project, the subsequent execution of the COPY command becomes necessary to incorporate those changes into the image. Essentially, Docker invalidates the cache for this specific layer when such alterations occur.

Dockerfile Layering

Arranging commands logically in your Dockerfile will reduce unnecessary rebuilds, therefore place resource-intensive steps near the beginning, and frequently change steps near the end.

Consider this example: a Dockerfile snippet that executes a Maven build using the source files located in the current directory.

```
FROM maven:3.8.3-openjdk-17-slim AS build

WORKDIR /app

COPY . /app

RUN mvn package

RUN mv ./target/demo-0.0.1-SNAPSHOT.jar ./demo-0.0.1-SNAPSHOT.jar

EXPOSE 8080

ENTRYPOINT ["java", "-jar","./demo-0.0.1-SNAPSHOT.jar"]
```

The current Dockerfile is inefficient, as updating any file triggers the reinstallation of all dependencies during each image build, even if the dependencies remain unchanged since the last build.

Optimization

Instead, it is advisable to split the COPY command into three parts. Firstly, copy the pom.xml file to validate the dependencies. Then, proceed to copy the project source code, which may encounter frequent changes, separately from the dependencies. This way, Docker will only rebuild the relevant layers, significantly reducing build time.

```
FROM maven:3.8.3-openjdk-17-slim AS build

WORKDIR /app

COPY pom.xml /app/

RUN mvn validate

COPY . /app

RUN mvn package

RUN     mv      ./target/demo-0.0.1-SNAPSHOT.jar
./demo-0.0.1-SNAPSHOT.jar

EXPOSE 8080

ENTRYPOINT    ["java",    "-jar","./demo-0.0.1-
SNAPSHOT.jar"]
```

By installing dependencies in earlier layers of the Dockerfile, you avoid the necessity of rebuilding those layers whenever a project file encounters changes. This approach helps save time and resources during image builds.

Hands on: Building a docker image

Build the Docker Image

If you do not have a workstation yet, scroll up to *Chapter 1: Provisioning Resources in a Private Cloud Environment* in order to set up one.

Then, connect to the Cloud9 environment you launched (**dev-infra**).

If you have not already cloned the project repository, go ahead and do so (Follow-up reference #6). Next, open your terminal or command prompt and navigate to the main directory of the project. Execute the following command in order to build your docker image:

```
cd ~/environment/

git clone https://github.com/naturalett/maven-workshop

cd maven-workshop

docker build -t my-web-app/single-stage -f Dockerfile.single-stage .

docker build -t my-web-app/multi-stage -f Dockerfile.multi-stage .
```

The docker build command builds a Docker image based on the instructions defined in the Dockerfile. The -t flag assigns a tag (in this case, my-web-app) to the built image.

The . (dot) at the end specifies the build context, which is the current directory.

By employing the multistage build, you will observe a difference in the sizes of the resulting Docker images. To verify this, execute the following command to compare their respective sizes.

```
docker images | grep -i 'my-web-app'
```

Chapter 6:
Deployment Strategies and Techniques - From Local to Production

In this chapter, web will explore deployment strategies and techniques, followed by building our Helm Chart deployment. This will equip us to efficiently provision and deploy applications within the EKS cluster.

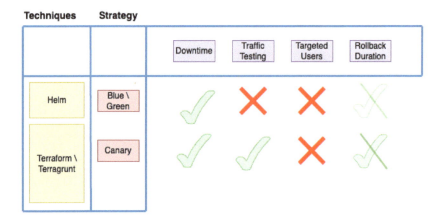

Run Docker on your local environment

In the world of software, updating and improving applications is something that always happens. To make sure these changes go smoothly and do not cause problems for users, DevOps teams use deployment strategies. These strategies are like different ways of doing things that help put new versions of apps and code into action. This way, companies can give out software updates in a smart and user-friendly way that keeps everyone happy.

But before we step into various deployment techniques and strategies, we will start by learning how to run our Docker container locally and we will push it to Docker Hub so it will be available for us later on when we will launch our Kubernetes Application.

Login to your workspace

If you do not have a workstation yet, scroll up to *Chapter 1: Provisioning Resources in a Private Cloud Environment* in order to set up one.

Then, connect to the Cloud9 environment you launched (**dev-infra**).

Docker Container walkthrough

Path: /

Port 8080

Earlier, we created the image by following the instructions in the *"Hands on: Building a Docker Image"* section. Now, let us make sure we still have that image. If you do not have the image, you can go back to the episode where we built the Docker image to create it again.

```
docker images | grep -i 'my-web-app'
```

Run the container

```
docker run --name my-web-app -d -p 8080:8080
my-web-app/single-stage
```

You can verify the operational status of your application by running the following command:

```
# Checkout that your container is up and
running

docker ps
```

```
# Send a curl request to your application

curl localhost:8080
```

Now, pause the container and shift to the next strategy -> Docker Compose deployment:

```
docker stop my-web-app && docker rm my-web-app
```

Push the image to Dockerhub

If you have not created a Docker Hub account yet, now is the moment to do so (Follow-up reference #10). Basically, it provides a centralized location to store and distribute your images to other developers, teams, or systems.

After setting up your account, proceed to log in to it:

```
docker login --username=<Your Username> --
password=<Your Password>
```

Subsequently, re-tag the prebuilt image to align with your organization's name and proceed with pushing it:

```
export ORG=<Your Organization Name>

docker tag my-web-app/single-stage $ORG/maven-
workshop

docker push $ORG/maven-workshop
```

Docker Compose

Additionally, we will run Docker Compose to showcase how multiple services can be combined and executed simultaneously. In this setup, we will use Docker Compose to launch our earlier hello world application along with a MySQL database, which will be on the same network. The goal of our application is to record a timestamp in the database whenever a user sends a GET request to the /healthcheck endpoint.

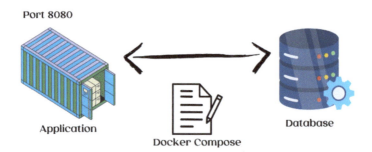

Let us take a brief look at our docker-compose file before running it:

```yaml
version: '3'

services:

  db:

    image: mysql:8.0

    container_name: maven-workshop-db

    environment:

      MYSQL_ROOT_PASSWORD: root_password

      MYSQL_DATABASE: healthcheck_db

    ports:

      - "3306:3306"

  app:

    build:

      context: .

      dockerfile: Dockerfile.single-stage

    image: my-web-app

    container_name: maven-workshop-app
```

```yaml
    environment:    #    Define    environment
variables for the app service

    - app.init-db=true # Set the value to
true

    ports:

    - "8080:8080"

    depends_on:

    - db
```

The docker-compose file is divided into two services:

1. The application is getting built from the local Dockerfile that is named Dockerfile.single-stage.
2. The second service is based on the MySQL 8.0 image.

We are exposing the application service on port 8080.

Run the docker-compose file

If you have not already cloned the project repository, go ahead and do so (Follow-up reference #6). Next, open your terminal or command prompt and navigate to the main directory of the project. Execute the following command to initiate the Docker image build:

```
cd ~/environment/

#                    git                    clone
https://github.com/naturalett/maven-workshop
```

```
cd maven-workshop

docker-compose up -d
```

Once the docker-compose completes building and fetching the required dependencies from the specified YAML, let us examine the status of the containers in our environment:

```
docker ps
```

Confirmation of the timestamp

Next, we will access our MySQL container to confirm the creation of timestamps corresponding to the clicks we make on the path localhost:8080/healthcheck.

Log into your MySql container (in a new Terminal session):

```
docker exec -it maven-workshop-db bash
```

Connect to the MySql (password is root_password):

```
mysql -h localhost --user root -p
```

Now, select your database and observe the table being created as we send requests to the endpoint:

```
show databases;
```

```
use healthcheck_db;

show tables;

SELECT * FROM healthcheck;
```

Submit a request to your container:

```
curl localhost:8080/healthcheck
```

Stop the docker compose

```
docker-compose down
```

Get ready to explore deployment strategies and techniques

Now that we have gained familiarity with running local Docker containers and using Docker Compose, it is time to delve into production deployment strategies within the orchestration.

Let us explore two main aspects:

1. **Deployment Strategies**: This will cover Blue/Green and Canary deployments.
2. **Deployment Techniques**: This will dive into application deployment approaches, including Helm deployment and Terraform/Terragrunt deployment.

Cloud

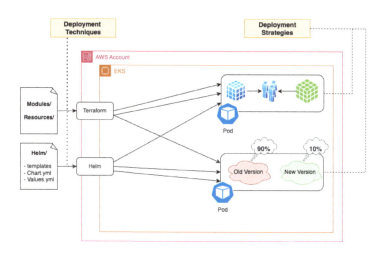

Local Machine

Deployment strategies

A Dual Version Strategy

A dual version strategy is known as the Blue/Green Deployment strategy that involves running the new version of the software concurrently with the outdated version.

This strategy offers a significant advantage in the form of rapid updates or rollouts for new application versions. However, it comes with a notable drawback of increased costs due to the concurrent operation of both old and new versions. Engineers often favor this approach in mobile app development and deployment.

Gradual Transition for Enhanced Stability

This strategy is known as the Canary Deployment. The deployment team introduces the latest version and progressively redirects production traffic from the old version to the new one. This technique involves maintaining a distribution where the older version handles a majority of traffic (e.g., 90%), while the newer version serves a smaller portion (e.g., 10%). By testing the stability with live traffic from a subset of end-users at different levels during production, DevOps engineers gain valuable insights into the performance of the new version.

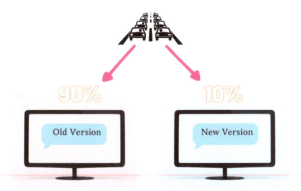

Canary deployment offers improved performance monitoring and facilitates faster, more reliable rollbacks in case of new version failures. However, it comes with the drawback of a slower and more time-consuming deployment cycle.

Deployment Techniques

Helm

Picture Helm as a smart container for your Kubernetes applications, simplifying their deployment like a well-organized toolbox. In this toolbox, you will find something called "charts," which are like pre-packaged sets of instructions for Kubernetes. Imagine you are constructing with building blocks – each chart is an organized collection of these blocks, where each block represents a component of your application, whether it is a web server, a database, or other parts. These charts are structured in a specific way, like arranging your building blocks in a particular order.

Now, when you want to share or use one of these "building block collections" (charts), you place it in a special folder. Think of this as placing your toolbox in a specific spot. But the magic happens when you use Helm, your virtual assistant. It takes the toolbox (chart) and follows the instructions to assemble your application on Kubernetes just the way we have described. It is like giving Helm a recipe and letting it cook up your application.

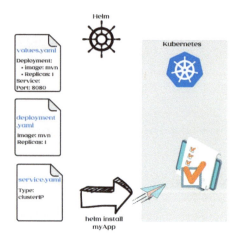

This process of using Helm and charts is incredibly useful because it ensures that your applications are consistently deployed across different environments. Whether you are setting up a small service or a complex application stack, Helm simplified the deployment process by managing the instructions and pieces for you. Just as you can upgrade parts of your Lego city without having to rebuild the entire thing, Helm allows you to make changes and updates to your application without having to start from scratch. So, in essence, Helm is like a reliable builder that helps you create and manage your Kubernetes applications efficiently, turning intricate setups into manageable and repeatable processes.

Terraform

Let us break down Terraform in a clear and simplified manner. Even though we have already used Terraform to set up a complete infrastructure, it is a great time to explore Terraform more deeply on a theoretical level. This way, you can gain a comprehensive understanding of the tool's advantages and strengths.

So, how does Terraform do its magic? It communicates with various computing platforms, such as clouds and services, by making use of specific files, kind of like writing down a recipe for tech stuff.

Think of it like having a unique key for each door. Here is the interesting part – Terraform has the ability to communicate with numerous doors, or in other words, interact effectively with a wide array of computing environments.

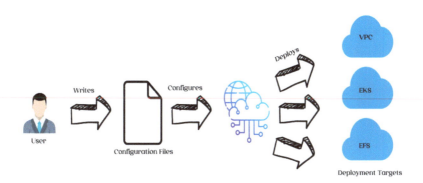

Terragrunt

Think of Terragrunt as your cloud journey's coding wizard. It saves you from writing the same code over and over – you write it once and use it anywhere.

But wait, there is more – Terragrunt is also a coding organizer. It is like a digital librarian that sorts your code into folders. And here is the cool part: Terragrunt lets you use the same set of rules in different parts of your code.

In simpler terms, Terragrunt is like a helper for Terraform, giving you extra tools to keep your code clean, work with different code pieces, and manage things smoothly.

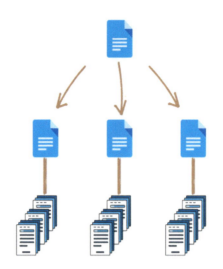

Deploy your first application in EKS using Helm Chart

Now that we are comfortable with deployment strategies and techniques, we can step into creating our Helm Chart deployment. This will allow us to provision and effectively deploy our application within the EKS cluster.

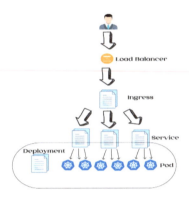

Our Helm Chart contains the following Kubernetes resource:

- Deployment: defines how your application runs.
- Ingress: acts as a traffic controller. It manages external access to your service.
- Service: enables internal communication between different parts of your application.

Login to your workspace

If you do not have a workstation yet, scroll up to *Chapter 1: Provisioning Resources in a Private Cloud Environment* in order to set up one.

Then, connect to the Cloud9 environment you launched (**dev-infra**).

Export the DNS of the preexisting Load Balancer

We will fetch the initial Load Balancer in your environment. If you happen to have multiple Load Balancers, please go to the AWS

Console and export the DNS of the applicable Load Balancer in your setup.

```
export LB=$(aws elbv2 describe-load-balancers
--query "LoadBalancers[0].DNSName" --output
text)
```

Clone the project repository maven-workshop (Follow-up reference #6) and deploy it.

```
# Clone the repository if you didn't do it yet

cd ~/environment/

#            git            clone
https://github.com/naturalett/maven-workshop

cd maven-workshop


helm upgrade -i hello-world \

    --set "namespace=default" \

    --set "text=Non Canary Deployment" \

    --set "canary.enabled=false" \

    --set "ingress.hosts[0].host=$LB" \

    --set
"ingress.hosts[0].paths[0].path=/hello-
world(/|$)(.*)" \
```

```
  --set
"ingress.hosts[0].paths[0].pathType=Prefix" \

./helm
```

Hands Up

Similar to what we accomplished with the Kubernetes Dashboard in the *"Provisioning a Kubernetes Dashboard"* section, we have two ingress annotations: "rewrite-target" and "configuration-snippet." These annotations modify our endpoint to /hello-world, enabling us to utilize the existing Load Balancer from the Kubernetes Dashboard. However, if you have your domain name, endpoint rewriting becomes unnecessary.

Final Check Ups

```
kubectl get pods -n default
```

In the meantime, you can examine the logs of the pod:

```
kubectl logs -n default $(kubectl get pods -n
default                                      --
selector=app.kubernetes.io/name=hello-world --
output=jsonpath={.items..metadata.name})
```

Check out your deployed service:

```
curl $LB/hello-world/
```

Clean up the environment:

```
helm del -n default hello-world
```

Configure a Canary deployment

That strategy will let us test new changes by directing a small number of requests to a different service than the main one. You can use the canary annotation in your Ingress specification to control this behavior.

NGINX Ingress Controller supports gradual traffic splitting based on the following order:

Headers and cookies can target a group of users with the new version, while weight reroute a percentage of traffic to it. Annotations like canary-by-header and canary-weight enable this.

Remember, canary deployments require two ingresses (regular and alternative), and only one canary ingress is allowed.

In our example, we set up canary traffic based on the user's region using the header. Additionally, we assign a weight of 40% to this configuration.

Login to your workspace

If you do not have a workstation yet, scroll up to *Chapter 1: Provisioning Resources in a Private Cloud Environment* in order to set up one.

Then, connect to the Cloud9 environment you launched (**dev-infra**).

Export the DNS of the preexisting Load Balancer:

We will fetch the initial Load Balancer in your environment. If you happen to have multiple Load Balancers, please go to the AWS Console and export the DNS of the applicable Load Balancer in your present setup.

```
export LB=$(aws elbv2 describe-load-balancers
--query "LoadBalancers[0].DNSName" --output
text)
```

If you did not do so, clone the project repository maven-workshop (Follow-up reference #6):

```
# Clone the repository if you didn't do it yet

#              git              clone
https://github.com/naturalett/maven-workshop

cd ~/environment/maven-workshop
```

Deploy Non Canary Version

```
helm upgrade -i hello-world-non-canary \
```

```
  --set "namespace=default" \

  --set "text=Non Canary Deployment" \

  --set "canary.enabled=false" \

  --set "ingress.hosts[0].host=$LB" \

  --set
"ingress.hosts[0].paths[0].path=/hello-
world(/|$)(.*)" \

  --set
"ingress.hosts[0].paths[0].pathType=Prefix" \

  ./helm
```

Deploy Canary Version

```
helm upgrade -i hello-world-canary \

  --set "namespace=default" \

  --set "text=Canary Deployment" \

  --set "canary.enabled=true" \

  --set "ingress.enabled=false" \

  --set "canary.hosts[0].host=$LB" \

  --set "canary.hosts[0].paths[0].path=/hello-
world(/|$)(.*)" \
```

```
--set
"canary.hosts[0].paths[0].pathType=Prefix" \

./helm
```

Hands Up

With the implementation of the ingress of the canary we are not just rewriting the endpoint to be hello-world we also have additional annotations for our canary:

```
annotations:

  nginx.ingress.kubernetes.io/rewrite-
target: /$2


nginx.ingress.kubernetes.io/configuration-
snippet: |

    rewrite ^(/hello-world)$ $1/ redirect;

  nginx.ingress.kubernetes.io/canary: "true"

  nginx.ingress.kubernetes.io/canary-by-
header: "x-region"

  nginx.ingress.kubernetes.io/canary-
weight: "40"

  nginx.ingress.kubernetes.io/canary-by-
header-value: "us-east"
```

Canary

This annotation indicates the implementation of a canary deployment strategy using the Nginx Ingress Controller in Kubernetes. Setting this annotation to "true" instructs the controller to direct a portion of incoming traffic to the new version of the application while continuing to send the majority of the traffic to the existing version.

Canary-by-header and canary-by-header-value

This annotation indicates that traffic routing depends on the "x-region" header's value in the incoming HTTP requests. Specifically, if this header contains the value "us-east". With this setup, a portion of the traffic is directed to a new application version, depending on specific header values like the geographic region from where the request comes.

Canary-weight

This annotation allows you to control the proportion of traffic that is directed to the new version of an application compared to the existing version. The annotation lets you assign a weight or percentage to the canary version, indicating the share of incoming traffic it should receive.

Let us check our Canary

With Header

You can send the header in your request and to check if it directs our request to the canary resource:

```
curl -H "x-region: us-east" $LB/hello-world/text
```

Expect output:

Canary Deployment

Reason:

We have the ingress annotation tag of nginx.ingress.kubernetes.io/canary-by-header

Without header

```
curl $LB/hello-world/text
```

Expect output:

Non Canary Deployment

Reason:

The request is routed through the initial service ingress, lacking the canary annotation.

Multiple attempts without header

```
curl $LB/hello-world/text
```

Expect output:

- Non Canary Deployment
- Canary Deployment
- Canary Deployment
- Non Canary Deployment
- Non Canary Deployment

Reason:

Because we have another canary annotation, which is the nginx.ingress.kubernetes.io/canary-weight. As mentioned, the annotation rules prioritize Header, Cookie, and Weight in that order.

Clean up the environment

```
helm del -n default hello-world-non-canary

helm del -n default hello-world-canary
```

Chapter 7:
Wrapping Up and Staying Engaged

In this final chapter, we will tidy up our created environment and provide you with links to stay updated on our innovative cloud solutions.

Clean up the Infrastructure

When it comes to cleaning up the infrastructure, it is advisable to reverse the order of creation. This is because there are interdependencies among the modules, and the output of each module is necessary for the subsequent steps.

Clean Up the Infrastructure module

Access your Cloud9 instance within the "Provisioning Resources in a Private Cloud Environment" section (**dev-infra**) and execute the following:

```
cd ~/environment/workstation/terragrunt/services/kubernetes-dashboard/

terragrunt destroy --auto-approve
```

```
cd ~/environment/workstation/terragrunt/services/ingress-nginx/

terragrunt destroy --auto-approve
```

```
cd ~/environment/workstation/terragrunt/infra/05-metrics-server/

terragrunt destroy --auto-approve
```

```
cd
~/environment/workstation/terragrunt/infra/04
-nodeGroups/managed-node-group/internal-
services/

terragrunt destroy --auto-approve
```

```
cd
~/environment/workstation/terragrunt/infra/03
-eks/

terragrunt destroy --auto-approve
```

```
cd
~/environment/workstation/terragrunt/infra/02
-efs/

terragrunt destroy --auto-approve
```

After Terragrunt removed all the resources you can go ahead and to delete the Cloud9 of dev-infra.

Clean Up the VPC

Access your Cloud9 instance within the *"Provision a VPC using Cloud9"* section (**dev-vpc**) and execute the following:

```
cd
~/environment/workstation/terragrunt/infra/01
-vpc/

terragrunt destroy --auto-approve
```

```
aws s3api delete-objects --bucket $BUCKET --
delete "$(aws s3api list-object-versions --
bucket $BUCKET | jq '{Objects: [.Versions[] |
{Key:.Key, VersionId : .VersionId}], Quiet:
false}')"
```

```
aws s3api delete-bucket --bucket $BUCKET --
region us-east-1
```

After Terragrunt removed all the resources, you can go ahead and to delete the Cloud9 of dev-vpc.

Deploy the entire infrastructure with a single command

We are delighted to offer you the ability to deploy the complete infrastructure with just a few clicks. Now, you can effortlessly launch the entire infrastructure as your playground, simplifying the process and enhancing your experience.

For the convenience of deploying multiple Terraform modules with a single command, we will use the `terragrunt run-all` command. It simplifies the Terraform modules as a stack and automates the execution of Terraform commands in the correct dependency order, making actions like deployment or destruction efficient.

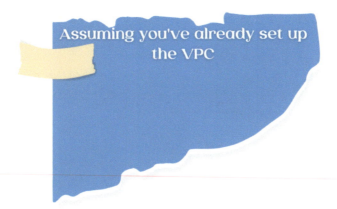

Assuming you've already set up
the VPC

Provisioning

Access your Cloud9 instance within the *"Provision a VPC using Cloud9"* section (**dev-infra**) and execute the following:

Infrastructure modules – EFS, EKS, Node Group and Metrics Server.

```
cd ~/environment/workstation/terragrunt/infra/

terragrunt run-all apply --terragrunt-exclude-
dir 01-vpc
```

Internal services – Ingress Nginx, Kubernetes Dashboard.

```
cd
~/environment/workstation/terragrunt/services
/
```

```
# Create the Load Balancer

terragrunt run-all apply --terragrunt-include-
dir ingress-nginx


# Allow AWS a few minutes to finalize the
creation of the Load Balancer resource

terragrunt run-all apply --terragrunt-include-
dir kubernetes-dashboard
```

Clean Up

Access your Cloud9 instance within the *"Provision a VPC using Cloud9"* section (**dev-infra**) and execute the following:

Internal services – Ingress Nginx, Kubernetes Dashboard.

```
cd
~/environment/workstation/terragrunt/services
/


terragrunt   run-all   destroy   --terragrunt-
include-dir   ingress-nginx   --terragrunt-
include-dir kubernetes-dashboard
```

Infrastructure modules – **EFS, EKS, Node Group and Metrics Server.**

```
cd ~/environment/workstation/terragrunt/infra/

terragrunt run-all destroy --terragrunt-
exclude-dir 01-vpc
```

Stay Connected

Thank you for joining me on this exciting journey through the realms of technology, DevOps, and Cloud solutions. Our learning adventure does not have to end here! There are several ways for you to keep exploring, engaging, and up to date on the latest insights and hands-on education that I'm excited to share.

YouTube Channel

If you are hungry for more visual demonstrations and in-depth explanations, make sure to check out my YouTube channel. I regularly upload short, practical tutorials and guides that complement the concepts we have delved into. Hit that subscribe button and never miss a moment of discovery!

https://www.youtube.com/channel/UCAL-GJzEiaf8PsbGmMy-KNA

Medium Profile

For a deeper dive into the world of technology and DevOps solutions, my Medium profile is where you will find detailed articles and blogs. Explore a wide range of topics, from infrastructure insights to coding complexities. Feel free to engage with the content through comments, shares, and discussions.

https://medium.com/@lidor-ettinger

DZone

Join me on DZone, a hub for all things programming and DevOps. I share news, tutorials, and tools that I believe will empower you on your journey. Stay tuned for the latest updates and join the conversation with fellow tech enthusiasts.

https://dzone.com/users/4878961/naturalett.html

Udemy Course - Continuous Integration and Jenkins Pipelines in AWS

Ready to take your skills to the next level? Join my Udemy course, where we dive deep into the world of continuous integration and Jenkins pipelines within the AWS ecosystem. It is a hands-on experience that will equip you with practical knowledge to excel in your DevOps endeavors.

https://www.udemy.com/course/hands-on-mastering-devops-ci-and-jenkins-pipelines-in-aws/?referralCode=0F32127B68008428C23F

Remember, learning is a continuous journey, and I am excited to have you as a part of it. Whether it is through videos, articles, or courses, there is always something new to explore and conquer. Let us continue to grow together, innovate, and make strides in the dynamic world of technology.

www.ingramcontent.com/pod-product-compliance
Lightning Source LLC
LaVergne TN
LVHW072049060326
832903LV00053B/299